Milo's Story

The cases I reveal in my books are all based on true experiences, but I have changed names and some details to protect their identities as they go on to build new lives and families of their own.

THROWN AWAY CHILDREN

Milo's Story

Louise Allen
with Theresa McEvoy

MIRROR BOOKS

MIRROR BOOKS

© Louise Allen 2025

Names and locations have been changed throughout in order to protect the identities of individuals.

The rights of Louise Allen to be identified as the author of this book have been asserted, in accordance with the Copyright, Designs and Patents Act 1988.

All rights reserved. No part of this publication may be reproduced, stored in a retrieval system, or transmitted, in any form or by any means without the prior written permission of the publisher, nor be otherwise circulated in any form of binding or cover other than that in which it is published and without a similar condition being imposed on the subsequent purchaser.

1

Published in Great Britain and Ireland in 2025 by
Mirror Books, a Reach PLC business,
5 St Paul's Square, Liverpool, L3 9SJ.

www.mirrorbooks.co.uk
@TheMirrorBooks

Print ISBN 9781915306906
eBook ISBN 9781917439237

Design and production by Mirror Books.

Printed and bound in Great Britain by
CPI Group (UK) Ltd, Croydon, CR0 4YY

Cover image: Alamy
(Posed by model)

This book was printed using
FSC approved materials.

MIX
Paper | Supporting
responsible forestry
FSC® C171272

For all the children who have been

Mistreated

Misunderstood

Misdiagnosed

There is no such thing as an attention-seeking child, only a child who isn't being listened to.

FOREWORD

The shame I felt strangled me. It was a snake around my neck, and someone else had wrapped it there.

As a child I was 'stupid'. I was 'shy'. I was 'troubled'.

What if we turn all these descriptions on their head and ask different questions?

I recently re-read a letter I wrote to my birth mother when I was nine years old. Carefully handwritten on lined paper, it was a polite, and perhaps, with hindsight, brave request for help.

My adoptive mother had moved my young birth mother into our home. If you have read my memoir, *Thrown Away Child*, you will already know this. I had two mothers in my home. I was terrified of offending anyone. So I tried to create sentences that did not use the word 'mum'. I was so distressed that I pulled out my hair and eyelashes. They thought I was mad. Both women stood in front of me and said, 'she's disturbed', neither recognising that they were the reason.

That experiment to get me back to my birth mother

failed. They went their separate ways with much dislike of each other. No one told me, and I was left dangling, thinking it was all my fault. I gathered pennies over a period of time and snuck out to buy a stamp from the village shop. I stole an envelope from a desk drawer. All the spelling mistakes are my own. This is what I wrote:

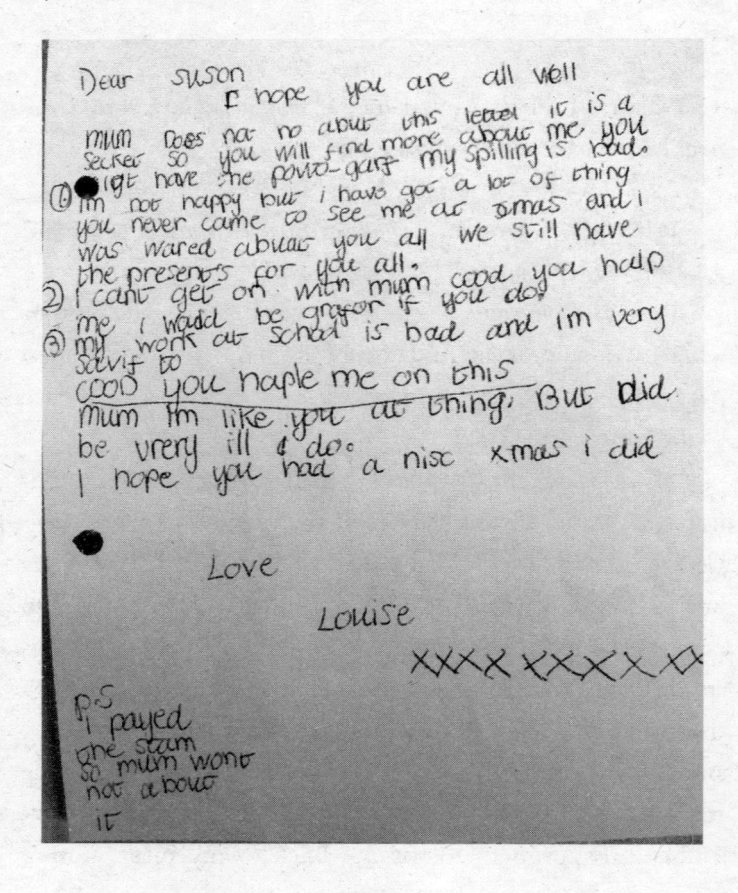

> Dear Suson
> I hope you are all well mum does not no about this letter it is a secret so you will find more about me you igt have the povto-garf my spilling is bad.
> 1) I'm not happy but i have got a lot of thing you never came to see me at xmas and i was waried about you all we still have the presents for you all.
> 2) I cant get on with mum cood you help me i woud be grafor if you do
> 3) my work at schol is bad and i'm very scrvif to
> cood you naple me on this mum I'm like you at thing. But did be vrery ill i do.
> I hope you had a nise xmas i did
>
> Love
>   Louise
>   xxxx xxxxx x
>
> P.S
> I payed the stam so mum wont not about it

In case you found that difficult to read, I have no doubt that I found it difficult to write. Here's what I think I was trying to say:

Dear Susan,

I hope you are well. Mum does not know about this letter. It is a secret. So you will find out more about me, you might have the photograph. My spelling is bad.

I'm not happy but I have got a lot of things. You never came to see me at Christmas and I was worried about you. We still have the presents for you all.

I can't get on with Mum. Could you help me? I would be grateful if you do.

My work at school is bad and I'm very sad. If you could you help me on this, Mum? I'm like you at things.

I hope you had a nice Christmas. I did.

Love Louise xxxxxxxxx

P.S. I paid the stamp so Mum won't know about it.

Of course, what I was really trying to articulate was the problem of having two mothers, something that Lily, our long-term foster child, also grapples with. I didn't know if my birth mother had received my letter until I read my file around 15 years ago. I found the letter and a drawing I had made of my birth mother and her son, my half-sibling.

What it demonstrates more than anything is just how confused and desperate I was.

Childhood can be a very confusing place.

Milo is the story of a little boy whose world was very strange and frightening – for all sorts of reasons that you're about to find out.

Sometimes we need to turn things upside down and look down the other end of the microscope so that we find a new angle.

How many children are failed by the adults around them because the right questions weren't asked?

PART ONE

Michelle

1

'Go on, then. What do you reckon to our chances today?'

Michelle and Andy are on their way to the match. The Rams have been in freefall since an away defeat on the first day of the season, so Michelle asks Andy the question tentatively. But the sun is shining and Andy is in a buoyant mood. He breaks off from humming the tune to *We are Derby* to answer her.

'Babe, it's in the bag. I've got a good feeling about today. We're going to smash them.'

Michelle smiles and puts her hand on his arm.

It's a little bit optimistic to describe it as 'in the bag', given the team's woeful start to this year's campaign, but now that they've been living together for three years, Michelle has come to know that Andy has the eternal and sometimes entirely unfounded optimism of the die-hard supporter.

His good mood only increases as they drive across the city.

The housing estate where they live is in a suburb on the other side of Derby from the football ground, and it would be far quicker to bypass the centre of town, but Andy likes to take the direct route to Pride Park, where he's more likely to spot other football supporters on the way. He drums his fingers on the steering wheel when they are caught by a red light at the corner of Midland and London Road by the old Crown and Cushion pub, a favourite haunt of his years ago. It's been closed for a while now, but back in the day it was a good meeting point to have a warm-up pint before a game.

'Had some good times in there over the years,' Andy says, as he always does when they drive past.

Before we knew each other, Michelle thinks, but doesn't say it out loud. Andy's life before they met is none of her business. She's distracted from thinking about pubs by a large advertising hoarding up ahead. This isn't the first time it's caught Michelle's eye. A washing machine dominates the image. The door of the drum is open and a woman's arms can be seen pulling laundry into a white, plastic basket.

The strapline reads, *Have you got room in your wash for one more pair of jeans?*

In the bottom corner there is more text. *You can earn up to £700 per week per child*, it promises. After that, in big letters, a contact number.

Michelle takes a photo.

'What do you think you're doing?'

On their way to a football match is not the moment to discuss her thoughts about fostering. But with Grace all grown up and one foot out of the door at university, Michelle is not relishing the empty nest. She has been thinking about fostering for some time.

'Nothing.'

Inside the stadium, Andy gets them each a coffee and they make their way to their seats. The same ones he's sat in since the club moved from the baseball ground in the late 1990s. It's a familiar aspect to Michelle, even though she's only been coming intermittently for a couple of years. Except that today something is different. There are adverts in every corner of the ground.

Have you got a big heart and an empty room? reads the one in the south east corner stand where the away fans sit. *All they need is someone to love them. Give a child in need a loving home*, reads another.

Michelle takes photos of each one. It's as if they are speaking directly to her.

She notices that the telephone numbers are different on each, which seems strange. Michelle has no idea how fostering works, but it seems that it isn't that straightforward. There are choices about the various routes in you can take, and different agencies and organisations are involved. Somehow she had imagined that it would all be centralised.

It's nil-nil at half-time.

'But we've definitely had the best of it,' Andy nods sagely as he gulps down his pint.

Michelle is distracted. She hasn't been caught up in the game like she usually is. 'Yeah, totally,' she says, before Andy launches into a monologue about a pattern of play on the left wing when they should have scored. 'That referee should have gone to Specsavers. We'd be one up if he had.'

Andy's optimism is well-founded. Derby do indeed score early in the second half and manage to hold onto the lead for all three points.

Andy is jubilant and insists on stopping for another couple of drinks on the way home. It's amazing the way the football result dominates the whole character of a weekend. Michelle is the designated driver on the way home but makes the most of Andy's chipper mood, seizing the opportunity to sow the seed that she has been carefully storing.

'Andy, I think we could foster.'

'Those bloody adverts. I knew what you were thinking as soon as you took that picture earlier! Look, it's not for us, love.'

'Hear me out. It could be for us. We've got two spare rooms now that Grace is at university, and she could sleep on the sofa bed when she comes home.'

'Like she's going to agree to that!' Andy scoffs, knowing his step-daughter well.

'But listen, Andy, we could make £1,400 a week if we

take in a couple of children.. Do the maths. That's £5,600 a month. That's getting on for £70,000 a year! Way more than my salary.'

Now Andy does begin to tune in properly to Michelle's conversation. He makes a disgruntled face. 'Are you serious? That's double what I earn.'

'It wouldn't take much. I've raised Grace. I know children. I can look after them. How hard can it be?'

Andy shrugs. 'You're the expert.'

'Yes, I am.' Michelle raised Grace pretty much single-handedly until she was 16. Andy hasn't had to do much parenting in the two years that he and Michelle have been together.

'Do they really pay that much?'

'They do. I've been looking into it. I could leave the town hall and kiss those long hours goodbye.'

'It's a thought.'

'It's more than a thought. It's an answer! It's easy, Andy. I mean, we could get a couple of little ones, couldn't we? I'd love a girl and maybe a little boy.'

'Steady on.'

But Michelle is in full flow now, so much so that she has to check her speed through town. The reading on the speedometer has drifted upwards with her enthusiasm.

'Andy, this is it. This is the answer to all our problems. If you carry on working while I do the fostering that would bring in nearly £100,000 a year between us. A household income in three figures. Imagine it! We could save some money for our retirement, buy another property. We could go on holiday.'

Andy is really paying attention now.

'Well, it's interesting, I'll give you that.'

After dinner, when Andy falls asleep in his armchair, Michelle continues her research. She compares all the websites that were in the adverts. One is a council one, and there are two other companies also seeking foster carers.

They seem to be competing in the same arena – literally. Michelle smiles at her own joke.

It takes a bit of time for Michelle to work out that the two companies are private companies, but they look much more impressive than the council option. She is drawn to their slick websites, the convincing Ofsted ratings and the superior financial remuneration.

The money really is great. One child can earn them up to £800 per week if that child has 'additional needs'. Nothing specifies what additional needs might be, but in Michelle's mind, that means dyslexic tendencies or ADHD. She knows she could do that, no problem. Her heart begins to sing as she pictures sweet little faces in her head: lines of orphan Annies arriving at their front door carrying battered suitcases, cuddly toys and a big smile on their grubby faces.

Her vision is fed by the websites. Picture after picture of beautiful, happy, white-toothed children, nourished and healthy. It doesn't occur to Michelle for one moment that these are stock images of children available royalty-free and often repeated on different private companies' websites.

She clicks on a video link. 'Becoming a foster parent is the most rewarding thing you can do,' beams a lady in jolly dungarees. She speaks in a sweet, childlike voice about how to become a foster carer. 'It only takes between four and six months to be assessed,' she assures her captive audience. 'All the necessary checks to safeguard our young people can be carried out with minimum fuss.'

All these words and images swirl around Michelle's head.

'We can do this. We'd be so good at it,' she murmurs out loud. She looks across the room to Andy, who is snoring contentedly in the chair. He's like a big, cuddly teddy bear with a good heart. He's been a decent stepfather to her daughter in the last few years. Her heart warms further as she pictures him with two little children on his lap, then kicking a ball around in the back garden while she brings out hot chocolate and homemade biscuits to their little family. There will be trips to Pride Park when they're bigger. Bonding over football. Days at the beach with hampers full of elaborate picnic food. Newly-painted bedrooms. Yes, a trip to IKEA is needed.

II

The following morning, Michelle wastes no time in taking action towards her new-found dream of fostering. She needs to push Andy while he's still feeling receptive, strike while the iron is hot!

Although each website emphasises the ease of the process, Michelle decides to email both of the independent fostering agencies, and the council, just to make preliminary enquiries. Something inside her tells her that the council is the right way to go, but at least this way she has all bases covered and has begun to put her thoughts and words from yesterday into deeds.

Even though it's a Sunday, within an hour of hitting 'send', one of the agencies is on the phone.

'Hi, Michelle, this is Angie. It's so great that you've taken this step, and I'm here to support you through each stage of the fostering journey. The first thing we need to do is make an appointment to see you in your home. How does Wednesday evening sound?'

Three days doesn't give Michelle much time to get the

house straight, but she is thrilled that things are happening already.

'Wednesday sounds perfect.'

As soon as she puts her mobile phone down, Michelle leaps into action. First, she sets about deep-cleaning the house from top to bottom. The usual drudge of housework feels good when there is such purpose behind it.

When Andy wakes up, he doesn't need much persuasion to start clearing the garage. Michelle's enthusiasm is infectious.

Clearing out the spare room is just a question of finding somewhere to store Andy's old football programmes. Grace's room doesn't take Michelle long either; Grace has taken so much of her stuff off to uni, and seems to take a little bit more each time she returns home for a visit. Those visits have become briefer and more infrequent. The room itself is quite bare. What's left behind is all the books and toys that Grace loved when she was younger but has now grown out of. Looking around gives her a pang of nostalgia for those days, but it also makes her feel excited for what is to come. These things will be perfect for a younger child and it's wonderful that they can be used again.

Yes. They are really going to make a difference to a child's life.

It would be nice to have a little boy, Michelle decides. She'd always wanted a second child after Grace was born. A boy would have made the pigeon pair. But the right man didn't come along until Andy, and by then it was too late. Not that Andy had wanted children when they met. But through fostering, they *could* have the pigeon pair. Or take two boys. Make a new little family.

Michelle hums as she dusts and sorts the room. She consciously removes anything too pink and girly and makes the room look more neutral. She takes a blue throw from the sitting room and repurposes it as a bedspread. It's fun imagining the children, the boy or boys who might live here. Initially, Michelle had pictured a little blonde boy. Maybe a brother or sister. Now her thoughts wander to refugees. Perhaps a black, Asian or mixed-race child. They could even take a Muslim child. It would be interesting to learn about another culture. It doesn't matter where the child comes from. They are doing a good thing. Giving something back to society. She won't mention race to Andy, who has been known to make the odd, inappropriate comment in certain company.

Several trips to the tip later, the house and garage are immaculate. Michelle suspects that Andy's motivation is more financial than benevolent, but still, they make a great team.

'It just shows what we can do when we put our minds to it!'

On Monday evening they take a trip to the Nottingham IKEA after work. It's open late and Michelle persuades Andy that they 'need' the cushions, lamp, plants and throws that she stacks the trolley with. They linger in the children's area and Michelle finds more bits to dress up Grace's old room and the spare room.

'I thought this was supposed to make us some money, not cost us,' Andy says.

Michelle puts her hand on his arm, but can tell that he's in good humour, buoyed along by her own zeal.

'It's not *just* about the money, Andy. We're doing this to change the life of a child. Or children.'

On Wednesday, Michelle finishes work early so that she can be totally prepared for what she perceives as an interview rather than an appointment. She goes through every scenario she can think of in her head, makes a list of all the questions she imagines they might get asked. She phones her sister who is a nurse.

'I think you're bloody mad,' is the first thing that Tracy says. Then she talks about her best mate who's a social worker. 'And she says that these kids will destroy your life!'

Michelle refuses to hear it all. They're kids. How bad can they be?

She spends a good 20 minutes doing an online search for prayer mats in case they do get a Muslim child. Some come with a compass in the corner so they can be sure that they're facing the right direction when they pray. She selects one and keeps it in her basket, just in case. Wouldn't do to jinx it.

By the time Angie from the agency is due to arrive, Michelle has plumped every cushion multiple times and their little three-bed terrace is transformed.

'Can't even sit down in my own bleeding house,' Andy mutters.

Michelle is curtain-twitching at every car that drives down their street in the hour before the allotted time. It's close to 6pm when she says, 'Bloody hell. A Tesla's just pulled up and parked along a bit. Do you think that's her?'

Despite theirs being a recent housing development, there is hardly anywhere to park. Cars are forced to park half on kerbs jammed along the roads. Most households have two cars, something that the architects appear to have forgotten to factor into the development.

A woman dressed in a black suit emerges from the car and heads towards the house. She wears dark sunglasses, even though dusk is descending. She carries a folder of paperwork under one arm and a black handbag clinks on a gold chain over the other shoulder. She looks– *impressive*, thinks Michelle.

She squeezes Andy's arm. 'Right. This is it. Best foot forward.' She flicks the kettle on just before she heads towards the door to let Angie in.

Bernie, their cockapoo, greets Angie enthusiastically, thrusting his nose into her skirt.

'Sorry about that! Don't worry, he's very friendly.'

Angie brushes invisible hairs from her immaculate suit.

'And he doesn't moult,' Michelle says, more pointedly than she intends.

After the initial chat, when Angie has assured Michelle that a dog is perfectly acceptable for foster carers, and the plate of Tesco's Finest biscuit selection is almost empty (mostly consumed by Andy), Michelle begins to relax.

Angie is as impressive in person as she is from a distance: a big personality. In other circumstances, a woman so commanding might rub Michelle up the wrong way, but Michelle warms to her instantly. Everything about her exudes class. Her expensive scent fills the house as she wafts her arms around, admiring their home.

'It's in a great location, this development. I didn't know they'd extended so far out this way. Your house took some finding. Lots of wriggly turns and cul-de-sacs on the estate.'

'Yes, it's quite a maze when you're not familiar with it.'

'Stylish, though. The architects have put some thought into it. I like the way that each house is a little bit different.'

Michelle and Andy's place is weatherboard wooden-clad, in between two stone-fronted houses that look more traditional.

'It gives them a bit of character,' Andy says, doing his best to join in with the conversation.

'Yours feels more "New England beach house" than Derbyshire cottage. I like it.'

'Come and have a look at the rest of the place,' Michelle says, taking Angie's cup from her. 'We've changed my daughter's bedroom around now that she's at university and has moved out, so that's created a second spare room.'

While Michelle takes Angie on a tour of the house, Andy hovers behind, working hard to play his part and put on the best show they can for Angie. Although Michelle is the driving force, all those trips to the tip mean that he's quite invested now. And feeling some of the 'virtue' that Michelle keeps alluding to.

As she shows Angie round, Michelle tries to see their home through a visitor's eyes. Even though they've done so much to spruce it up in the last few days, Michelle can see so many other areas of potential for improvement. She is already mentally spending some of the fostering income she anticipates.

Angie compliments their taste as she looks in each room. She nods at the spare room and, when they reach Grace's recently repurposed bedroom, she looks around, appraising the size of the space. 'Yes, this is good. Really good. Actually, with bunk beds or even twin beds, I think you could get two siblings in here, if you wanted to.'

Another £800 per week. Another £42,000 a year on top of what they've already calculated. Michelle looks at Andy who shares a raised eyebrow and a smile in return. It almost feels like winning the lottery. At this rate, they could be one of the couples on the estate that has two cars.

By the time they finish the tour, showing off the bathroom with its new IKEA bamboo accessories, the two toilets, one up, one down, and the back garden, 'fully fenced in and with space over here for a small trampoline,' Andy is imagining a new 4x4 to move them all about, and also considering reducing his hours at work. Or actually, maybe not. If he kept his job they would be into three figures annually.

Michelle is likewise dreaming fast. In her vision of the future they are not only rich, driving nice cars, but they are adored in the community for their benevolent good works and are acquiring a modest property portfolio. By the time they are back in the kitchen and Angie is handing out glossy information leaflets, in Michelle's head they are the best carers the agency has ever seen and she is contemplating early retirement in Spain with a handsome pension and an MBE.

'Are you looking at any other agencies, may I ask?'

Michelle has a momentary panic. What's the correct answer here? 'Um, we've contacted the council,' she admits.

Angie nods and smiles, unphased.

'And you also contacted another agency, didn't you, love? They're coming tomorrow,' Andy pipes up.

Michelle shoots him a warning look. She doesn't want anything to go against them when they're so close.

'That's great. I hope it goes well for you,' Angie smiles even more.

Michelle breathes out a little sigh of relief.

'But I can see that, without doubt, you are the right people for us. You have a beautiful home, and I can tell how committed you are. In fact, I don't mind saying that you're exactly what we're looking for.'

Michelle's heart does a little leap.

'You could foster three to four children comfortably,' Angie continues. 'Two sibling groups or even a group of four siblings.'

The financial return on *four* children in their home would be enormous. The numbers are too big for Andy or Michelle to fully calculate.

Then Angie drops the big one. 'So, if you come to us, we'll offer you a £3,000 bonus. What we like to call a golden hello. You just need to sign here.'

When Angie departs, Andy forgoes his beer and joins Michelle in a celebratory glass of prosecco while she cancels the other agency's visit.

'We should get used to this,' he says with a wink, as he clinks Michelle's glass. Neither of them takes a moment to wonder whether or not this is all too good to be true…

Within an hour, an email from Angie is in Michelle's inbox. First thanking them for choosing their agency, Angie then outlines the next steps in the process.

The next steps involve them undertaking a series of 'Skills to Foster' courses, after which there is the introduction of the social worker who will take them through the Form F assessment; a process that explores 'whether you're right for fostering, and whether fostering is right for you'.

But from what I've seen this evening, I imagine that this will be a mere formality, Angie finishes. *It was great to meet you. You're going to make great foster parents!*

For the next few days, Michelle and Andy stay up on cloud nine, firmly believing that their lives are about to change forever.

How right that prediction would turn out to be.

III

A few days later, the introduction to Michelle and Andy's 'Form F supervisor' arrives via email. She is called Elaine and, 'has some space in her diary a week on Thursday, just to get the ball rolling'. Michelle is itching to get things underway as soon as possible, but a week on Thursday will have to do.

Elaine could not be more different to Angie. Instead of a shiny red Tesla, she arrives in an old, silver-blue Ford that has seen better days. At some point it has been clipped on the rear left side, leaving a crumpled door and bumper. The driver's door has been touched up with paint that doesn't match the rest of the car. Elaine herself *does* seem to match her car. She is – yes, there is no other word that comes to Michelle's mind other than 'scruffy'. She is a scruffy-looking woman. Her wire-brush hair sticks out in strange directions. She wears a white shirt which Michelle judges must have been washed with blue jeans at some point, giving it a strange, blueish tinge that definitely wasn't the manufacturer's intention. Her bottom half seems to not quite match with the top, almost like she is a character in a game of consequences where one person has drawn the legs on without seeing what the player before has sketched. Ballooning Aladdin trousers are totally incongruous with the rest of her outfit. She has a scrubbed face with veins showing in her red-toned cheeks, in marked contrast to Angie's perfectly smooth foundation.

'Good morning to you both.'

Elaine speaks with a clipped accent that Michelle can't place, but feels a long way from the soft Derbyshire burr that most people around here have. Where Michelle warmed immediately to Angie, in fact, if she's honest, wanted to emulate her, she's not even sure she wants to invite Elaine into their newly-revitalised home. Still, with her eye on the three-figure prize, she will swallow her prejudices and avoid ruffling any feathers. Elaine gets the royal treatment, just as Angie did.

Elaine's questions are very different from Angie's praise.

'How do you do your recycling?'

Michelle is a little thrown by that, but overplays their environmental credentials. 'We compost all our peelings and I'm on a drive to reduce our use of single-use plastics.'

She then underplays their alcohol consumption when Elaine wants to know how much they drink in an average week. When Elaine lifts the lid of their recycling bin, the prosecco bottles from after Angie's visit still sit on the top, above Andy's beer cans.

'Oh, those are from our neighbours, Sue and Frank.

They had a family party at the weekend and asked if they could use our bin.'

Elaine seems satisfied, although Michelle blushes at being forced into the lie.

The visit seems to be going well. They progress rapidly through the first few pages of this Form F nonsense. Michelle is Applicant 1, Andy Applicant 2. Verification of identification documents, employment history and details of household finances are tedious, but straightforward. However, when they are each asked to provide the contact details for their respective ex-partners, things feel a little less comfortable.

'Right. And is that really necessary?' Andy asks, before Michelle shoots him a warning look.

'It's standard procedure,' Elaine says. 'A normal part of the safeguarding check.'

Michelle herself is on reasonable terms with Phil, Grace's father. She explains to this irritating woman intimate details of her relationship, about how they met through work, about Phil being 20 years her senior. How they discovered that they actually had very little in common once Michelle found out that she was pregnant. How they separated amicably and Grace has regular contact with her father. Andy has met Phil many times because of Grace, and he knows these circumstances well, so it's familiar territory and doesn't seem too intrusive, initially. Besides, Michelle's relationship with Andy is sound. They're each too long in the tooth not to have baggage, and Andy's heard all of this before. There's no need for jealousy. But then Elaine asks lots more questions, probing each response deeply. She seems keen to explore how these realisations and feelings might affect her ability to foster. How does Michelle feel about her 'failed' relationship now?

'But it was all such a long time ago. Grace is 19! Does it matter?'

Michelle is shocked by the way that everything that comes out of her mouth is pounced upon and twisted, then cross-examined by Elaine. It feels more like an interrogation than an interview. The initial feelings of dislike she felt for Elaine intensify, but she knows that she has to put up with it. She has a word with herself, tries to view it all as if it's a gruelling interview for an incredibly well-paid job. Which it is. *Think of the money*, she reminds herself.

Then it's Andy's turn to provide contact details for his exes. Because he wasn't with Sue, his previous partner, for very long, he also has to give the names of the two relationships he'd had before her, giving the dates when the relationships ended. It's an uncomfortable situation. Michelle hasn't heard him mention the name 'Rosie' before. She wonders why not. Does Elaine have any idea how difficult this is, to talk about ex-partners in front of the current one? It almost feels designed to cause friction.

Andy is asked to comment on his parenting experience, given that he doesn't have any children of his own. As well as supporting Michelle with Grace for the last couple years, he talks about his experiences with Rosie's children. 'I often looked after her kids, took them to school. Even took them to Legoland when she was away with her girlfriends.'

This is all news to Michelle, who tries not to look nonplussed in front of Elaine, but wonders why they've never talked about it before. How did she not know about Rosie and her children? Why would Andy hide that?

The atmosphere in the room becomes even more uncomfortable when Elaine asks them about their sex life. She seems unperturbed by the direction of her questions, as if it's perfectly natural to ask two people who were strangers until just a few moments ago where and when they have sex.

'And would you say that you make a lot of noise during lovemaking?'

'Um, no more than, um, average,' Andy says.

Michelle almost laughs out loud. How the hell is one supposed to assess 'average' in this instance?

Now it's Michelle's turn to ask if all of this is absolutely necessary.

'It's not personal. It's all just designed to make sure that this is a suitable household to bring children into. We ask everyone.'

Michelle is beginning to get more than a little fed-up with the Form F process. This time it's Andy who gives *her* a placating look.

She thinks again of pound signs and the promise of a better life.

'And do you perform any sex acts that involve bondage or swinging?'

Andy spits out his coffee. 'No. N.O. No.'

'And Michelle, do you participate in *Only Fans* or similar?'

Michelle has no idea what *Only Fans* is.

Andy does, though. 'Are you on there, yourself?' he asks Elaine with a sneer, before he can stop himself.

'It's part of my job to check every potential foster carer's social media.'

'You can't really call that social media, can you?' Andy blurts out, before Michelle sends him another warning frown.

'Well, that's as much as we can do before the first stage is complete,' Elaine says eventually, much to the relief of Michelle. 'I'll be in touch once the references are through, so that we can complete the Form F process.'

'There's more?' Andy asks, incredulous.

'We've done most of Section A. There are five sections to the form though. It generally takes 4-6 months. Could be quicker, could be longer. Depends.'

Elaine doesn't elaborate about quite what it 'depends' on, but Michelle is too frazzled by the meeting to follow up.

When Elaine finally departs, leaving Michelle smarting over the various things she's discovered about Andy during the meeting, the mood in the kitchen is still raw. Michelle can't help bringing up the subject of Rosie. 'It just seems odd that you've never mentioned her before. Or her children!'

Inevitably, perhaps, given how bruised and anxious they

both feel, the 'discussion' escalates into a row. It all feels like such a violation of their relationship. Andy's response is to mow the lawn at speed. Michelle heads out to the supermarket to find something to buy to calm down, even though they have already been shopping for the week. She buys a prawn cocktail mix, with an iceberg lettuce and a French stick. Back at home she makes herself a sandwich, not offering one to Andy. In all the time they've been together she's never done that before.

It's as if they've let something new, unwanted and potentially insidious into their home and their relationship.

It takes several more weeks for the references to come back, by which time the frost in the domestic air has had a chance to thaw. Michelle is relieved when they get the confirmation that all the references have been accepted. Asking her employers for a reference is fair enough, but she didn't enjoy the business of asking friends for a personal reference commenting on her parenting skills.

There are more meetings scheduled with Elaine, with even more questions to answer. Thankfully, none of them are as excruciating as the first one. Michelle and Andy persevere, jumping through every hoop that is put in their way, even if they sometimes do it through gritted teeth.

'It's all designed to put people off,' Andy says. 'I bet loads drop out before they get to this stage.'

'Not us, though.'

'Not us.'

But, just when they think they are almost there, at the final meeting with Elaine, and immediately before they are scheduled to go to 'panel', Elaine announces that she is going to interview the ex-partners.

Andy visibly pales.

For a moment, Michelle wonders if he is ill, then realises that it's because he looks horrified. Elaine must see it, too.

'Is there any problem with that, Andy?' Elaine asks, sharply. 'Is there a particular reason you don't want me to speak to-' she looks down at her notes, 'Let me just check. Ah, yes, Rosie?'

'No. There's no problem,' he says, a little colour returning to his cheeks. 'Ask away.'

Michelle isn't convinced.

'Are you *sure* you're okay with her interviewing Rosie?' she asks, once Elaine has gone. 'You didn't look too happy about it.'

'In for a penny,' he shrugs.

'In for more than a penny,' Michelle reminds him. *Think of the money* has become a kind of mantra at each hurdle that has been put across their path.

'Yeah,' he says, with an unconvincing smile. Michelle wonders what it is he's hiding.

Another few weeks go by. Michelle and Andy complete their Skills to Foster course, and become friendly with another couple that they meet on the programme. They hit it off with Graham and Theresa during the sessions and swap numbers so that they can stay in touch. It's good to know that someone else has gone through the same things they did. They manage to laugh over the Form F stuff, but only once they're outside in the car park, away from the social workers and agency representatives.

'All those questions about the exes!'

'It was an absolute nightmare!' agrees Theresa. 'I don't mind saying that we actually had a bit of a row afterwards.'

'So did we! How funny,' Michelle says.

'And then when they got onto our sex life,' Andy joins in.

'What?' said Graham. 'We weren't asked about that, were we?'

Theresa shakes her head. 'No. We were asked about sexual orientation at the start, but not about our actual sex lives!'

Not for the first time, Michelle wonders if Elaine has abused her powers in some way, but once again she takes a deep breath and keeps her mind on the money.

Meanwhile, Elaine has a problem tracking down Rosie for the interview, which delays things even further. The suggested 4-6 months turns into eight months. Elaine seems obsessed with seeing each and every one of the exes and family members listed on the form, even driving to the other side of the country to interview Grace at university.

'So I'm afraid we're going to have to delay going to panel until I've managed to speak to this Rosie in person,' Elaine says on the phone.

Andy seems relieved that Elaine can't get hold of Rosie, but also anxious that they shouldn't fall at this final hurdle. 'Jesus. She's spoken to everyone. What does it matter? We've come this far. She knows my inside fecking leg measurement. Isn't that enough?'

Michelle is thoughtful. 'I'm going back to Angie. This is ridiculous.'

Returning from the supermarket, Michelle pulls a packet of expensive chocolate chip cookies from her shopping bag, ready for the meeting with Angie.

'Four pounds for six cookies? Are you having a laugh?' Andy blows out his cheeks to remind Michelle that when this is over and they have been to panel, 'we're straight back on multi-packs for 90p'.

Angie, who seems to have eyes and ears everywhere and sometimes acts more like some kind of mob-boss than a fostering agency manager, agrees that the delays and Elaine's investigations are ridiculous and unnecessary, and promises to step in to support Michelle and Andy.

It's been a gruelling eight months... and it isn't over yet.

IV

All of a sudden, with intervention from Angie, things start moving.

'I've had a word with the chair of the panel who unanimously agreed with me that there were enough references. They don't see the point of delaying the panel just to wait for one more, so we'll stick with the date next week as arranged,' Angie explains by phone a few days later.

'Excellent! Elaine will just have to suck it up,' Andy says, with some glee, once Michelle is off the call.

After all the months of waiting and hoping, panel day is upon them. They meet with Elaine once more so that she can explain who will be there, and exactly what they should expect.

'Make sure you get a good night's sleep before the day. And brush your hair and teeth before you go.'

Andy laughs along at Elaine's joke. Michelle notices the sharp look Elaine returns him. It seems it wasn't a joke.

On the day itself Andy is quite relaxed, even though

Michelle has convinced him to wear a suit with a white shirt. 'It's good to look like the people who work at the fostering company. Like we already work there.'

'I'm not wearing the tie,' Andy grumbles.

'You don't have to wear the tie. All the male managers have a certain look about them. Have you noticed? They wear suits with white or blue shirts, but open collar and no ties. The women in management all wear black. Angie's always in black. And very smart.'

'Unlike the social workers.'

'Well, Elaine seems to be a law unto herself, but yes, they generally seem more relaxed.' Michelle appraises Andy when they are ready to go, straightening his jacket before she nods in approval.

'You'll do.'

'I didn't realise I was living with Hyacinth bloody Bucket,' Andy says.

'I just want to create a good impression. I'm modelling us on that couple who are splashed all over the leaflets and the homepage of the website.'

'We've spent the best part of a year trying to create a good impression.'

'And we're not going to ruin it now.'

'If the panel chair asks you to strip naked and stick a rose in your bum, I reckon you'd do it,' Andy jokes.

'I would if she thought it would help us become the foster carers that we have spent so long trying to be!'

In their car on the way to the panel they are both quiet and overly polite. Almost as if Angie and the panel are sitting in the back listening. Inside her head Michelle has 'please like me, please let this go well,' on repeat. It helps to imagine that they aren't sitting in the slightly rusting Volkswagen Polo, and instead are driving their new 4x4. Probably a black one, thinks Michelle.

When they arrive, well before the appointed time, it isn't just Michelle and Andy in line. There are lots of other new foster carers also going through the process. Graham and Theresa are having their panel interview on the same day. They wish each other good luck and promise to let each other know the outcomes. Each panel interview is scheduled to last around an hour. Elaine is there to support Michelle and Andy's application, as is Angie. Elaine seems to have gone quiet today. There is not a peep from her about what they should or shouldn't say. Michelle wonders if perhaps Elaine is intimidated by Angie. On one hand, it seems unlikely that Elaine would be intimidated by anyone. But there's definitely tension. A 'them and us' feel in the waiting room.

Michelle is nervous. This is the culmination of everything they have been working towards. There is so much at stake. But, at the same time, she knows that there is no way they can fail. They have practised for the interview for weeks. They've done all the research and know roughly what questions are likely to come up. As if rehearsing for a play, they have been running through their answers while cooking and eating dinner each night. In the event, their preparation stands them in good stead.

'Why do you want to be a foster parent? What motivates you to foster?'

Their answer has nothing to do with making money. In fact, Michelle is careful not to mention money at all. Instead, she talks about wanting to 'give back' to the community now that they're in a position to do more since Grace has moved on to uni.

'How have you found the assessment process?'

They don't say things like 'intrusive' and 'uncomfortable', which is what they really feel. Or 'potentially damaging to our relationship'. 'Borderline abusive'. There is quite the list if they were honest.

Instead, they reply carefully with the sensible, slightly unreal self-righteous answers that they learnt in Skills to Foster, making sure to back each other up to show how in tune they are – with the process and with each other. Andy mostly remembers the lovely buffet, but Michelle was a diligent student and took it all in. Her crib notes have served them well.

Since the course she has also done more reading about trauma and ADHD. She knows all the theories of attachment and her knowledge of safeguarding is as up-to-date as it could possibly be.

When the questions become more intense, Michelle takes the lead.

'What would you do if your foster child refused to go to school?'

'We know that it won't be easy. Given the circumstances that lead to a child entering the care system, there are bound to be challenges like this. We've thought about it a lot, and we think the most important thing is trying to understand why they don't want to go to school. Once we've got to the bottom of that, we can set about finding the best way to help. I think we'd try positive incentives next. They might work, depending on the age of the child and the specific circumstances…'

She launches into her planned responses, using the royal 'we' as often as she can, knowing that she has everything covered in a way that Andy doesn't, quite. She can talk for both of them. In her head it's as if she can *see* the child that they will be given after today. A mixed-race child would be best. She can show off to her family and neighbours. She'll learn how to do corn braiding like they saw in the Caribbean on holiday. It will be wonderful.

The hour is up. They are asked to wait outside while the panel discusses their suitability with Angie and Elaine.

More than 15 minutes tick by as they wait to hear the outcome.

Eventually, Angie comes out, wafting the long black sleeves of her dress like a bat in the belfry. She's all smiles and shakes both their hands.

'I'm delighted to tell you that you passed!'

Michelle and Andy are thrilled. Michelle makes a little squeal. Andy breathes a sigh of relief.

'That's the hard part done. Now all we need to do is to wait for the independent decision maker to review and agree. Then there is a 28-day wait for ratification and, at that point, you will begin your lives as foster carers. We'll have the first referrals waiting for you in just over a month. Congratulations!'

'Thank you so much for all your help!'

The dollar signs pop inside Michelle's head. Little does she know that the decision has just added £200,000 to the value of the fostering agency. Angie has six foster carers going to panel today, and if they all get in that's a million pound ticket for the agency. Michelle and Andy's dream of wealth is nothing compared to the financial ambitions of the company.

'Let's go out for dinner tonight,' Andy suggests when they are back in the car park and he can take his jacket off.

'Great idea. We've got lots to celebrate! And now we can really start planning the next stage of our lives.'

Michelle books a table in a restaurant they haven't tried before. 'We can afford to push the boat out a bit, now that we know our financial troubles are over,' she says, when Andy raises an eyebrow at her choice.

Next it's time to share the good news with Grace. After some initial grumbles about losing her room, Grace has been supportive about the idea of them becoming a fostering family. Having grown up as an only child, the thought of younger siblings is appealing.

'At least one sister, please,' she jokes down the phone. 'A baby one!'

'We don't know what ages or genders yet,' Michelle reminds her. 'And don't forget, we've agreed to foster from birth to 18. We might get someone closer to your age!'

'Hmm. Not sure how I feel about that. It would be weird to have someone nearly my age in my room.'

'Your *old* room!'

'I didn't realise I'd be leaving it for good when I packed up my stuff,' Grace says, but her tone is light-hearted. 'And you'd better not forget about your number one daughter.'

'My clever number one daughter away at university? How could I ever forget about her? What a role model your new sisters – or brothers – will have.'

On the way to the restaurant Andy seems preoccupied. Not surprising, perhaps. There is a lot to think about now that the dream is becoming a reality. Between courses, Andy leaves the restaurant a couple of times to vape. The main dining area is glass-fronted and Michelle can see him pace backwards and forwards outside the front of the building, vape plumes rising in his wake. She wonders who he is on the phone to. Probably sharing the good news with friends.

When he returns to the table, he is even more cheerful than he is after a Derby County win. He rubs his hands together as the steak is placed in front of him.

Michelle can already feel a shift. The prospect of having a wonderful new life, looking after children while making a load of money is changing them both. But something about Andy's behaviour is unsettling. She can't put her finger on it, but things are different.

Over the next few evenings, Andy is back home from work later than usual. Each night Michelle is desperate to talk about the latest reading she has done, or to share the stories she's heard from other foster carers, or to talk about something she's bought for the children's rooms. Elaine has urged them repeatedly to try to leave the rooms as a blank canvas, 'so that a child can put their own stamp on it,' but Michelle can't help herself. Her days are spent in eager anticipation of their first fostering arrival. It reminds her of all those years ago when she was excitedly waiting for a new baby, wondering if Grace would be a boy or a girl. There is that same impatience to meet this new little person. Not just whether it will be a boy or a girl, but also wondering what heritage the child will be. There is so much to talk about. It's frustrating when he isn't home on time. On the third day, Michelle challenges him. 'What's going on?'

'Nothing's going on. I'm just getting as much as I can done now so that I'm ahead of the game when the children start coming. If I tie up these few bits and pieces then I can help more at home when you need me. Now, what's for supper?'

Andy expressing a desire to be more involved with the general childcare is a sentiment that should please her.

Michelle suppresses the bubbling doubts. She feels mean for thinking that something might have been wrong. Andy is working hard for her and their soon-to-be new family.

Michelle shows him the latest IKEA purchases. New matching towel bales in bright colours.

'Don't you think you should hold back from spending any more money until the fostering allowances start to come in?' Andy says.

'I just want to make their rooms as special as possible so that they feel welcome,' she says.

'Especially since you've now given your notice in. I still can't believe you did that without us discussing it properly.'

'Well, you heard the man on the panel! I was just doing what he suggested.'

One of the panel had been a retired head teacher. He had asked Michelle if she had plans to leave her job since it would be beneficial for one carer to be at home, even if their foster children were school-aged.

'I just think it was a bit premature before we've had the independent decision-maker approval. And before we know where we are with finances.'

'Are you having second thoughts, Andy? Because we're not turning back now.'

'I'm just saying reign it in a bit, that's all.'

Michelle can't understand why there is tension between them at what should be a joyful time. She can't shake the feeling that there's something Andy isn't telling her.

V

After another 28 days waiting for the independent decision maker's approval, Michelle and Andy finally get the green light. They are clear! It's all systems go to fostering central.

Except that the phone doesn't ring, and the referrals don't fly in.

After a few more weeks of twiddling her thumbs at home having served out her notice at work, Michelle emails Angie to see what the hold-up is. It seems ridiculous that there are children needing homes when they have spent so much time – getting close to a year now – making their home ready and politely asking 'how high?' every time they have been asked to jump. She doesn't phrase her email quite like that, but makes her frustrations evident.

Nothing comes back for a few days, then Angie replies. *It can be slow at the start, but don't worry. Something will happen soon.*

Michelle has been checking in regularly with Theresa, her fellow foster carer friend from Skills to Foster. Theresa and Graham have received a referral for a girl aged 17 years.

That's great! Michelle replies.

No it isn't. It's for a 17-year-old girl, her boyfriend and their new baby...

Oh! Well, that could be fun.

When Michelle meets up with Theresa and another new foster carer, Fiona, for coffee, she is surprised at how exhausted her friend looks.

'It's just an awful lot of work for very little reward,' Theresa explains.

'What do you mean? Aren't you getting the pay they said we would?'

'Yes, we're getting the promised £800 a week, but we're barely seeing any of it. I've got to pay for all the nappies on top of food and clothes for the parents and the baby. We've had to find, and pay for, a buggy, a baby seat for the car, a cot, and all the other stuff I'd forgotten babies need.'

'But can't you claim back for that sort of stuff?' Michelle asks, aghast.

'Not according to Angie. That's what the allowance is for, apparently. Graham paid for everything up front and kept receipts but the agency aren't having any of it. I reckon we're worse off than we were before they arrived.'

'But that's not what we were led to believe,' Michelle frowns.

'Angie suggested that we found the items at car boot sales instead of buying things brand new, but it's been so busy and the baby just needs things when it needs them. It can't wait until the right thing comes up on Facebook Marketplace. It's not realistic.'

Michelle notices the baby has remained 'it'.

Fiona, who went to panel a few months before Michelle and Theresa, has a similarly bleak outlook. 'Luckily, I didn't give up my job as a dental nurse, although that was the plan initially.' She explains that she and her husband have been offered a bit of respite work for a couple of weekends.

'Respite work?'

'Right now we're looking after a girl whose foster carers need a break from her at weekends. So we have her two days out of seven. The fee is rubbish. It only works if you don't go anywhere that costs money or eat anything while you're out. We're out of pocket because we took her bowling and then went to McDonalds.

We spent the whole first weekend trying to please her. We drove to the nature reserve for a walk, because we were worried that she felt dumped. She thanked us by drawing all over the bedroom walls, which we now have to decorate. So, like Theresa says, doing respite has actually cost us money.'

'Wow.'

This is nothing like the dreamy picture Michelle had envisioned. When she gets back from meeting Theresa and Fiona, Andy is home uncharacteristically early. He tries to instigate another row.

'What do you think you're doing sitting around drinking

coffee while I'm slogging away trying to earn enough money to keep us both?'

Andy has become increasingly worried about money as the time has gone on. With hindsight, perhaps jacking in her job before they'd secured a placement wasn't the best idea she'd ever had. Still, Michelle has a new secret that makes her not answer Andy back for once. In all the boredom of being stuck at home, she has met someone online. It's all very innocent. Richard is miles away. He works on an oil rig. Nothing untoward has happened, they're just talking. But Michelle enjoys the distraction, given that Andy is out at work more and more, and argumentative when he's home. He only wants to talk about what a mistake they've made, or criticise her for not working, or for not doing more around the house.

They are both deep into their overdrafts, and the next mortgage payment is imminent.

A referral, however, is not.

And Michelle can't seem to get hold of Angie these days. She has stopped returning calls and emails, or fobs them off with empty platitudes. Michelle feels more than a little resentment for the woman who led them to believe that they would be instantly rich and have a lovely life. She suspects that she and Andy have been taken for a bit of a ride. She certainly feels like a mug. All that effort. All those hoops to jump through. All the pretence. All the expense! They've ploughed so much money into the home improvements, and without the income from Michelle's job they've had to nibble away at meagre savings. But they have come so far. They can't abandon the dream now.

Another month goes by and still there is no sign of placement.

Michelle distracts herself by keeping up the online flirtations with Richard. After all, what harm can it do? When she's not messaging him, she continues to bombard Angie with texts, emails and phone calls. They remain mostly unanswered. Not like when they were in the early stages of their application, when nothing was too much trouble.

As resentment builds, Michelle and Andy return to the pattern of rowing more than ever. Andy is still working longer hours and is away much more than ever before.

'Someone's got to pay the bloody bills!' he snaps.

But he's also out with his mates more than he used to be, too. Spending the extra money that he's supposedly earning on drinks in the pub. Drunk and angry one night, after a session with some of the boys in his local he lashes out. 'Fucking fostering bollocks. They sold us a five-star luxury hotel, but what have we got, Michelle? We've got a ripped fucking tent in a muddy field next to the motorway, that's what.'

'What are you talking about tents and hotels for?'

'I'm trying to show you what a fucking con it all is!'

Eventually, when Michelle emails Angie to explain that they are now being forced to consider 'other options', the phone rings.

'Great news,' Angie begins.

'A referral?'

'Almost. We've assigned your supervising social worker in advance of the first referral. She'll contact you to visit you at home.'

'Why don't we have a referral yet?' Michelle persists.

'We do have lots of referrals coming in, but nothing suitable for you as yet. These are not objects, Michelle. They're children. It's all about the matching.'

'Matching? What does that mean? There are no other children in our house to *match with*!'

'It's a host of other things, too. Proximity to their school, for example. The dog makes it difficult in some cases.'

'This isn't how you said it would be. You told us Bernie wasn't a problem.'

'Trust me. You're very close. We'll have something soon, I promise. Meet with Emmanuela, your supervising social worker, and we'll get you a referral.'

VI

More than a year after the football match where they made the fateful decision to embark on the path to becoming foster carers, they finally hear something. Michelle clicks on the link to the referral for a young boy called Milo. The picture shows a small, blonde-haired boy, seated against a white background. He is wearing a navy T-shirt over blue jeans. His fringe hangs down into his eyes.

Michelle's first response is one of overwhelming disappointment.

He's so very *ordinary*. A typical, white, council-house kid. Nothing at all like the tragic refugees she has imagined herself saving. In her mind's eye, perhaps inexplicably she has always pictured dark hair. Dark eyes. A swarthy child. Maybe mixed heritage. Instead, this Milo is nondescript. Mediocre. Nothing distinguishing him whatsoever. Boring.

She doesn't know what she expected to feel – perhaps some immediate maternal connection, but nothing like that happens.

She tries to have a word with herself. At this stage it really feels like beggars can't be choosers. Michelle has no idea that some unscrupulous agencies use this technique of 'starving' their foster carers to get them to accept placements that local authority carers would not take.

It's unrealistic, perhaps, but she expected to have a bit of choice in the child they'd take in. On the other hand, she reminds herself that this is what they signed up for and, right now, they really, really need the money. Perhaps it can just be a bit of practice for the real thing. If they take this 'Milo' for a short placement, she can get a feel for fostering – and show the fostering agency that she's a natural.

Michelle calls Theresa to run the referral past her.

'I would get out now, while you still can,' Theresa advises. 'It's not worth it.'

'But this is what we've been waiting for!'

'I honestly wish we'd never got involved. It's just not what you think it's going to be. We've given in our notice. The teenage parents and their baby are leaving at the end of next week. And we're not going to foster anymore.'

'What why not? What's happened?'

'It's all the stuff I was telling you about. It's actually *costing* us to be foster carers rather than generating income.'

'Maybe in the first instance. But surely the expenses will stop. I mean, I know you said you had to buy a lot of stuff initially, but once you've got it all, things will settle down.'

'Yeah, but it's non-stop. There's always something. And

they've just totally taken over the house. It will be a relief to get our home back, frankly. Honestly, none of it has been worth it.'

In spite of Theresa's warnings, Michelle feels that her only option is to accept the placement. They can't sustain their current financial arrangements.

She shares the news with Andy when he comes home.

For once, Andy isn't shouting. He sits down to read the referral form over and over again.

There's not a lot in it, but what is there is sounds fairly tragic.

Milo's parents were both drug addicts. His father's heroin addiction means that he is not able to parent, and his mother died of an overdose. There were no other family members who were suitable to look after him. Milo has been in care for a year, but his previous foster carers were elderly and not able to continue to properly care for a child of Milo's age as their own health deteriorated.

'Jesus, Michelle.' Beneath the gruff exterior, Andy has a big heart. He repeats out loud the bit about Milo's mother being dead and then his first foster carers not being suitable. 'What a story. If his parents were addicts then his home life would have been really unstable. We've all seen *Trainspotting*! And then to lose his mother! That poor lad.'

When Andy says all this, Michelle suddenly begins to see Milo as a real person rather than a disappointing photograph. She imagines a frail, old couple in a bungalow somewhere with a sad, hurt boy. She feels guilty for thinking about money first. And feels even more guilty about Richard the oil man when she sees Andy's sad face.

Andy looks back down at the referral. 'I mean, look at this bit. His birth wasn't registered so they've had to estimate his birthday. Imagine that! Parents too drug-addled to even get him a birth certificate. Poor lad. Imagine not knowing the date of your actual birthday! I thought that sort of thing only happened in Victorian novels.'

'And what would you know about Victorian novels, Andy?' Michelle smiles. 'Have you suddenly gone literary on me?'

Andy shakes his head and looks up at her. 'It's shocking, Meesh. Poor little fella! We've got to help this kid.'

It's decided.

Andy goes straight upstairs and starts to rearrange the bigger bedroom. They'd painted it neutral, but now he decides to paint one wall blue, where the bedhead goes.

He heads back out to B&Q for a pot of blue paint and it's done in an evening. 'It's just how my room was when I was a kid.'

Michelle can see that Andy is smitten. He's already seeing himself as this boy's dad.

'We're going to give him back his childhood, Meesh,' Andy says, with all the conviction of someone intent on being the best dad in the world.

The next day he goes to Sports Direct and buys a new

football along with some sports items in what he imagines to be roughly Milo's size.

Andy has totally bought into the idea of Milo as part of their family.

Michelle feels ever more guilty by the hour, but somehow it doesn't stop her talking to Richard on WhatsApp. She takes their cockapoo, Bernie, for more walks than he needs so that she can chat to him as she walks around the big park. Anyone watching her would see the way that she giggles like a teenager at Richard's jokes.

She loves his accent. Richard is from 'all over' in his words. His mother was American, his father was from Norway and he has lived in both countries. He tells her that he is taking early retirement and thinking of moving to Scotland. He has made so much money as an engineer that now he just wants to enjoy the rest of his time with a good woman. He plans to use his skills to set up a veterans' engineering project to do humanitarian work in developing countries. The foster caring life she previously envisioned that culminated in early retirement in Spain with a handsome pension and an MBE is rapidly being replaced by the picture of a life with Richard in Scotland. Possibly in a castle. Dreaming of wearing tartan and welcoming his relatives from Norway and America goes a long way towards explaining why she is still talking to Richard when she knows full well that she shouldn't. She can't help herself.

But the reality is that Milo will be arriving shortly.

The next step, now that she and Andy have said yes, is done through Emmanuela, their new supervising social worker. Emmanuela is Italian and rather flamboyant. She does a lot of gesticulation with her hands when she talks. Annoyingly, she only works three days a week, which means there are constant delays in communication.

Back at home she tries to draw from Andy's energy to rediscover the right mindset for the new arrival. She pulls out a new pack of blue sheets decorated with footballs from the landing cupboard. Milo will have a lovely room and all will be well in their world. After the slow start to their fostering journey, they will get siblings for the other room and the money will start to roll in. This is the life she has chosen.

So why does it feel so hollow?

VII

'Milo Day' is upon them. Michelle wakes early with some trepidation before making final checks around the house. Andy has taken the day off to be there for the welcome. He isn't due to be with them until late afternoon, but they are both anxious that everything should be perfect for his arrival. Emmanuela gets to the house a bit before Milo, who will be brought over to them by his own social worker, Annabelle. She sounded about 14 when Michelle spoke to her on the phone.

Emmanuela is less domineering than she seemed at their first meeting. Or perhaps they're just getting used to her theatrical way of speaking. She arrives with a packet of biscuits that Andy soon tucks into. He's nervous.

'How's Angie?' Michelle asks, by way of making conversation when there is an awkward pause.

'Sunning herself in the Bahamas,' Emmanuela says. 'The management team at the agency are enjoying a five-day cruise around the Bahamas, celebrating the company's record profits.'

'Are they, indeed. That's nice for them.' After another pause, Michelle asks, 'Why aren't you there?'

'Ah, well, I'm just a social worker. We don't hang out with the management team.' Emmanuela goes on to explain that there are management teams from different parts of the country all drinking champagne together on board.

'And buying their new Teslas,' Michelle observes, ruefully.

'And Jags and mansions,' Emmanuela joins in.

'Do they have foster carers in Scotland?' Michelle asks, thinking of Richard.

'No. Scotland and Wales don't do private social care.'

Andy pipes up, 'I bet they do. They probably just use a different vehicle for the money.'

Emmanuela looks genuinely perplexed. 'It's interesting that you say that. I was asked to travel to Wales to meet new carers a little while ago. I thought it was strange, knowing that the government banned private fostering and residential care.'

Andy, burnt by the experiences of the last year and now deeply cynical of fostering despite being invested in the idea of Milo, has more to say. 'That's so their governments can…' he breaks off and frowns. 'What's it called when they *pretend* to care?'

Michelle shrugs, confused.

'I know, it's called virtue signalling.'

Michelle looks at Andy, somewhat surprised by his insight.

At that moment, the doorbell goes. Andy has changed it to the original Batman theme for a laugh. Emmanuela looks bewildered by the 'na na na na na na na na' sequence, but Andy is up and at the front door before Michelle can even stand up. Bernie starts barking at all the commotion, and Michelle tries unsuccessfully to shush him while Andy welcomes Milo and Annabelle into the house.

Andy holds out his hand to shake Milo's, as if they're being introduced at a board meeting. 'Great to meet you, mate. Come through to the kitchen.'

Milo appears in the doorway behind Andy, and Michelle gets a first glimpse of him while trying to restrain Bernie. Milo is a bony little boy, with very pale colouring. His grey-blue eyes dart nervously around the room and he dances from foot to foot, apparently unable to keep still.

Annabelle troops in behind him and does, indeed, look very young. She has tattoos visible on her neck and arms and is wearing trainers. It's not a very professional look. Michelle finds herself making an internal tut of disapproval.

Nevertheless, she remembers her manners. 'Come and sit down, Milo. I'm Michelle. Pleased to meet you. Welcome to our home. Your home,' she adds.

She indicates a high stool next to the island and Milo climbs up onto it. He looks even smaller than his seven years. Emmanuela has done some checking but there really are no birth records. The grandfather hadn't even known about the boy's existence until the mother died and he was contacted by social services trying to track down his son.

Andy pushes the plate of biscuits so that it sits right in front of Milo, who looks carefully at all the adults. His legs continue to jiggle, even though he's sitting down. He's a bundle of nervous energy.

'Is there anything to bring in for Milo from the car?' Andy asks.

'Oh yes. Thank you, I'd forgotten. There's a bin bag full of his stuff in the car. Just a minute.'

Andy rolls his eyes.

'Do you need a hand?'

'No, don't worry. It's very light.' Andy nevertheless follows her out to help fetch in Milo's things. He needn't have bothered though, because Annabelle wasn't joking. The bin bag isn't even half full.

'Is that it?' Michelle says. 'Where are all his clothes?'

'He'll need new clothes. You know the circumstances, I think. The previous carers did their best, but I think they became increasingly housebound and that meant that not all of Milo's needs were being met. Don't worry, though. If you keep the receipts you can claim for some of them.'

Michelle remembers Theresa and Fiona discussing how much it was costing them to foster, and doubts very much whether they'll be able to claim anything back.

Andy looks as if he's about to speak, but before he can

say another word, Annabelle, who hasn't taken the proffered stool, starts to gather herself to go. 'That's me, then.'

'Is there nothing else we need to?' Andy begins, but Annabelle is already backing away towards the door. 'I'll see you out,' he manages to say.

With Andy momentarily gone from the room, Michelle doesn't know what to say or do. Now that he's here in the flesh, she has no idea how to interact with this boy in her kitchen. Thankfully, Emmanuela steps in and talks to Milo.

'It must all feel very strange, I'm sure. That's totally normal. But look at this nice house that you will be living in.' She fills the silence with her Italian exuberance, which is a good job, because Andy looks as shell-shocked as Michelle feels when he returns.

'She didn't even want to see his room,' Andy mutters.

Michelle suddenly gathers herself to take charge. 'How about I show you the garden, Milo?' she smiles, brightly. 'There are lots of things you can play with out there.'

Emmanuela stays in the kitchen with Andy while Michelle and Milo step outside. Immediately, Milo finds the football that has been bought for him. He kicks it straight back in the direction of the kitchen. It bounces against the wall just below the window and rebounds in Michelle's direction. Michelle picks up the ball and moves it to the other end of the garden. 'Shall we play down at this end?' she says, placing the football back down on the grass at a much safer distance from the house.

Milo looks down at the ball and takes a run up. This time his aim is better. He kicks the ball hard at the kitchen window, this time smashing the glass.

'Oh!' Michelle is too shocked to say anything else. It was such a deliberate and provocative action on the part of Milo.

Andy and Emmanuela come rushing outside.

'Uh oh, that's not going to be cheap to replace,' Emmanuela observes.

'No. Can we claim for it?' Andy asks, uncertainly.

Emmanuela makes an apologetic face. 'Unfortunately not. It will have to come out of your allowance. Sorry,' she shrugs.

Michelle, who by now has moved towards the house but has her eye on Milo, persists. 'Can't we claim it from the local authority?'

Emmanuela laughs at that. 'It's business. The agency needs to keep the LA happy, so no, you won't be able to get anything back that way. I'm sure you can claim it on your household insurance, though, no?'

She picks up her bag. 'I'll leave you all to get settled then. I'll see myself out and I'll call you in the morning to see how the first night has gone.'

Michelle is only half listening. Milo isn't bothered by the shattered glass. He's busy running around the garden, kicking over the flowerpots and climbing up their young trees, breaking branches as he goes.

He is a tornado.

VIII

Andy patches up the broken window with cardboard and tape as a stop-gap until they can get hold of a glazier, while Michelle clears the debris from the kitchen and prepares a snack. Milo, meanwhile, runs up and down the stairs over and over again. He seems to have unbound energy, in spite of his diminutive size.

'What are we going to *do* with him?' Michelle says, her words coming out almost as a wail.

'Give him time. It's a strange situation for him. We'll take him for a walk in the park to help him let off some steam. At least he can't break any more windows there, eh?' Andy's good humour is beginning to grate on Michelle.

The walk around the park is wild. Andy turns it into a chasing game, but it isn't really a game because Milo appears to seriously want to run away from them. Michelle is exhausted when they return.

It's a wrestle to get him into his new pyjamas – a gift from Grace that she has paid for out of her scant university funds.

She's due home at the weekend to meet her 'new brother'. Michelle takes his clothes straight down to the washing machine. They stink of cigarettes. They're tatty too, but will have to do until she can get him some more.

Settling him down for bed seems impossible. As soon as they leave him, he's up and out of the bed again, thumping around his room. When Michelle goes in for what feels like the 27th time, he throws the new TV on the floor and starts to laugh, darting past Michelle onto the landing and running around the house once more.

'It's probably just nerves,' Andy says. 'He doesn't know where he is. It's an unfamiliar environment. He'll settle down soon.'

They get very little sleep that night. Milo eventually collapses onto his bedroom floor in the small hours of the morning and Michelle puts his football duvet over him and lets him be, terrified that if she tries to move him he'll wake up and it will start all over again.

When they call Emmanuela the next day, she dishes out platitudes. None of it is helpful or placating. 'The first night is the hardest. He's settling in. It's all very new for him. He doesn't know where he is. Give it time.'

While Michelle is on the phone, Milo finds a sharpie and draws all over the wall that runs up the stairs.

'I'll take him over to the fields with the football so he can let off some steam this morning,' Andy says.

'How much more bloody steam can he have?'

But the space is welcome. Grace is arriving back this morning to meet her new brother, so Michelle can go to the station and pick her up. That way she can pre-warn Grace and give her a proper heads-up about what she's about to encounter.

'I've bought him a T-shirt. I wasn't sure what to get him.'

'Oh, love, you shouldn't be spending your student loan on presents.'

'I wanted to.'

'He might not be exactly what you're expecting,' Michelle says.

Unfortunately, no amount of pre-warning can prepare Grace for the fact that, after lunch, Milo punches her in the face and calls her a c***.

It's a very fraught day. Grace takes her rucksack and jumps straight back on the next train north. 'And I'm not coming back again until that little freak has either settled in or gone!'

But 'settling in' doesn't happen.

It isn't just the emotional strain. The household was already under financial pressure before Milo's arrival. There is no sign of the 'golden hello' that was promised, though Angie assured them it would be deposited within a matter of weeks. On top of having to buy Milo a whole new wardrobe to replace the tatty fragments that he came with, now each new day brings more broken things that need repairing or replacing: furniture, windows, ornaments.

Shelves are pulled away from walls. Crockery is smashed. Doors are kicked in.

'I don't know how we're going to afford to cover all this damage,' Andy frowns.

Worse is to come. Michelle and Andy console themselves with the fact that they will have some respite at least for the hours he's in school. But, when they approach the local primary, the headteacher finds an excuse not to take him.

'Unfortunately, under the circumstances, we're just not equipped to deal with his level of need.'

Neither are we, thinks Michelle. But how would the headteacher know that? Perhaps she can see something in his file that they didn't receive.

Within a fortnight, Michelle is utterly exhausted. The bulk of responsibility falls to her. After taking some time off initially, Andy is back at work and taking on more hours than ever in order to cover the mortgage and all the extra expenses. He's as worn out and stressed as she is.

'And no, I'm not taking him with me to the football. He can't sit still for five minutes, and that's my one bit of solace in the week.'

There is no respite for Michelle, even at the weekend.

Nothing is forthcoming from Emmanuela in response to their pleas for help. She came across as so domineering initially, but Michelle is fed up with the way she just bats away all the issues that are raised. There is no 'supervising' from their supervising social worker. A wet rag, Michelle decides. Angie is entirely elusive. She seems to be on holiday after holiday and never answers Michelle's emails or returns her calls. Michelle tries to engage with Annabelle directly, Milo's young social worker. But Annabelle makes complaints about *them* in return.

Meanwhile, Milo continues to terrorise the home and the community. It's impossible to take him anywhere. In the park he is violent towards other kids. Michelle feels awful about taking him anywhere in public, knowing that it won't be long before he creates a scene or causes some damage. It's easier to have him at home, where the damage is only to them and their things. It's less mortifying.

It doesn't take long before Michelle reaches the end of her tether. They're in a living hell. Everything is falling apart. With nowhere else to turn, she decides to email Ofsted. Although she's always just associated Ofsted with school inspections, Theresa reminds her that they are in fact, the Office for Standards in Education, Children's Services and Skills. Children's Services are not servicing the needs of this child, therefore she feels that her appeal to them is justified.

Suddenly there is action.

There is no response from Ofsted, but Angie turns up at the house, along with the regional operations manager. However, none of it is supportive. The opposite, in fact. They are very angry with Michelle; they wave complaints from Annabelle at her and Andy. 'You need to do more training. It's not Milo's fault. Perhaps you aren't cut out for fostering after all. Maybe I was wrong about you.'

But still no one has a plan for Milo. So, after another month of chaos and no support, Theresa's advice to them is, 'Do what we did. Just submit the 28-day notice. It's a straightforward process. At least you'll get your home back and can start rebuilding.'

Michelle does it immediately. Angie is incensed when she receives it and comes to the house. It's a last-ditch attempt to make them retract the notice. The meeting doesn't go well.

'This isn't fair on Milo. You haven't given the placement a chance! You're destroying his life!'

'But he's destroying our lives. Our home is a disaster area!'

Michelle has her head in her hands when Andy tells Angie to 'eff off'.

'Foster carers are quite disposable, you know,' Angie snarls.

Now the agency crank it up. The last thing they need is reputational damage. In a matter of days, the tables are turned on Michelle and Andy.

Angie returns to their house on Saturday morning with a manager from the local authority and a 'regional manager' who they've never met before. Michelle considers not letting them in, but Angie tells her on the front doorstep, 'I've got some information that you're going to need to hear.'

Michelle doesn't offer them a drink. It already has an

adversarial feel – of three against two. Andy is home from work for once. Angie turns her laptop around and shows them both an email from Theresa's fostering friend, Fiona. Fiona has 'raised a concern' about the nature of the relationship between Michelle and Richard, the oil rig man.

'Which is very serious indeed, because it jeopardises the safety of Milo. You know that we have to be very careful in our checks from a safeguarding perspective, and you never mentioned him on any of the application forms.'

Michelle feels utterly sick. She'd talked about Richard when she, Theresa and Fiona had gone for coffee. She can't even remember what she said. It had been fun to confide in relative strangers. Now she learns that she has been completely stabbed in the back.

'Your friend suspected that Richard might be a con man, so she got in touch with us and we were obliged to investigate.' Angie seems to be enjoying herself.

'I'm afraid to say that she was right. He is a con man. He has a long history of taking money from unsuspecting female lovers.'

'He's not my…' Michelle starts to say, aware that she must have turned bright red. She can't bring herself to look at Andy. Then she's angry. Why didn't Fiona tell her of her concerns, rather than the agency?

'Bitch,' she mutters, under her breath.

'I'm sorry?' Angie says. 'That's not the kind of language we expect to hear from our foster carers. Sadly, I'm afraid it's a repeated pattern in this house. Andy also swore at me the last time I was here,' Angie says, for the benefit of the managers. She shrugs and pulls a, 'but what can you do?' face. 'They're just not in a fit state to foster. Frankly, I'm not sure how they got through the panel interview.' Even though Angie has practically declared them incapable of fostering, it's made very clear that they will still have to look after Milo – who is running around the house as they speak – for another three weeks while they try to find another placement.

Andy has been silent for the last few minutes while the revelations about Richard have been shared. Now he shakes his head. 'Jesus, Michelle.'

Then, quicker thinking than Michelle, Andy asks about the £3,000 'Golden Hello' that they are still yet to receive.

Angie sneers, 'I don't think so.'

'I'm afraid that they're as bad as each other. Do you remember that we were unable to locate the ex-partner of Mr Webster? We made a mistake in not following that up.'

Angie then proceeds to share the email history of communication between Rosie and Andy. 'Mr Webster has also been, ahem, playing away from home, it seems.'

Andy is also snookered.

IX

The next week is tense. At no point has Milo's behaviour 'settled'. Michelle has just become accustomed to expecting disaster and destruction. He doesn't listen. He doesn't respond. He has no social skills. He barely speaks except to bark out demands, like 'cheese sandwich'.

There's none of the nice family life that Michelle once expected, recreating her motherhood days when Grace was little. Instead they play a daily game of damage limitation, moving any object that might be a target for his anger out of the way. Michelle has given up asking him to stop doing things.

'Milo, would you mind putting that down?' has absolutely no effect on his behaviour. In fact, he sometimes runs in the opposite direction with whatever it is.

'Milo, stop!' is equally futile. He doesn't seem to have any regard for material objects. Anything that could be broken now stays in a high cupboard. Pictures, photographs, clocks and ornaments have all been boxed away. The house is a shell in comparison to how they once lived. Milo doesn't seem to be particularly interested in any of the toys or books they've bought him. There is no way of getting him to sit down to do anything that might pass for school work. It's difficult to gauge his educational level in terms of reading, writing or maths, because anything paper-based that's put in front of him is just scribbled on. Michelle can't communicate with him because he doesn't really speak. Instead, he communicates by maniacal laughter whenever he destroys something. Mealtimes are fraught. Michelle has bought plastic plates for them all to eat from after losing too much Denby China in the first few days.

She wakes up each morning, assuming she has managed to get some sleep, with a knot of dread twisting in her stomach, compounded by the humiliation of discovering Richard's true intentions and thinking about how foolish she was in falling for it. She's bruised by thinking about Andy having an affair, even though she was on the verge of infidelity herself. There is no chance to clear the air. Andy is never present and, if he does come home, does little to help because he's 'exhausted after a day at work'. Any attempt to talk to him results in a row.

It is hell. Days are not spent living, but surviving. Getting through the next hour. The next day. The next night. Milo has taken to smearing poo on the walls and using the stairs and doorways like a gymnasium. Some days, Michelle lets it all rage on around her, locking herself in the bathroom until he calms down. On the days when she feels more able to cope,

Michelle spends a lot of time driving, going to open spaces that are further and further away from the house so that they spend longer and longer getting there. Strapped into a car is just about the only time when Milo isn't smashing something up.

So, at the end of the week, when Andy announces that he's leaving her, Michelle feels nothing. She can stay in the house. He will move in with Rosie.

Which leaves Michelle entirely alone with Milo, serving out the final three weeks of the 28-day notice.

With Andy gone, Grace still refusing to come home, and escalating debt, Michelle's life could not be more different to the happy family she'd envisioned. Her credit cards are maxed out to their limits and she has no way of paying off the debt. She can't go out to work while Milo is still here. It's impossible.

There is no support from Milo's social worker. Annabelle has moved on and a new one has been assigned but they are yet to make contact. It's a total mess. When Michelle is honest about her feelings, she realises that she has grown to despise Milo. It is as though everything is his fault. The break-up of her relationship with Andy, her desperate financial situation, her broken home.

When she thinks about it all, Angie also comes in for blame. And the hit list grows. That another foster carer, someone who should have been an ally, was responsible for reporting her to the agency is a bruising betrayal of trust. Theresa is guilty by association with Fiona. There is no one to turn to. There is no getting away from the fact that she was foolish about Richard, but otherwise, she feels that she – and Andy, in her more generous moments – have been wronged. The way they have been treated feels like a total violation. The most intimate details of their lives have been laid bare for public consumption.

Michelle is done with fostering.

She just needs to find a way to endure the next few weeks until Milo is gone. She has taken to leaving a plastic tray and bowl of food in Milo's bedroom and running away, rather than persevering with trying to get him to eat at the table with her. She buys packets of sandwiches and crisps because it's easier. She counts down the days until his departure, resolutely crossing them off on the calendar each evening once he is down for the night, typically around midnight, once he's worn out. Still often sleeping on the floor of his bedroom rather than the bed.

Weeks gradually turn into days. Soon the whole, horrendous experience of fostering will be behind her forever.

Except that it isn't. At the end of the 28 days, still no alternative provision has been found for Milo.

'Just a few more days,' turns into another two months.

Lonely and desperate, Michelle resorts to setting up an account on *OnlyFans*, the site that she'd never even heard of before she made the fostering application.

Finally, an email arrives from the fostering agency. A new carer has been found. At long last Michelle will be free of Milo.

PART TWO

Louise

I

'Why don't we give some thought to having another foster child? We've had a good break for a few months. Might be about time to welcome someone new?'

Lloyd raises an eyebrow from the other end of the dining table. The children are seated between us, plates of spaghetti bolognese being cleared rapidly.

'Yeah,' sniffs Jackson, the oldest of my birth children.

'S'pose,' agrees Vincent, his younger brother, with a shrug.

'But no more nut job girls!' finishes Lily. This isn't terribly charitable from her, a foster child herself. I notice that her make-up is much more dramatic than it used to be. She's entering another phase of teenager.

Milo's Story

To be fair, though, I'd already been thinking about a boy, someone younger than these three, who has a different lifestyle and needs. My crew are young teenagers and we seem to see less and less of them now that they're growing up so fast. They're much more likely to spend time hibernating in their rooms than socialising with us. I can just about entice them down with food, but the days of all watching a film, or going to the park, or playing a game together are fast becoming a distant memory. We don't seem to do any real running around with them any more. (Although we most certainly still do a great deal of running around *after* them.)

We think of Lily as a long-term foster child. She's been with us for a number of years, though not long enough to have learnt to use a napkin, evidently. I shake my head with a smile as she uses the heel of her hand to wipe bolognese sauce from her chin. It matches the rather dark shade of lipstick she's wearing. I'm describing her food as 'bolognese' sauce, but we're eating a vegetarian version with Quorn and lentils instead of mince to accommodate Lily's complicated dietary needs. ('Complicated' in the sense that for a vegetarian she still eats remarkably few actual vegetables.) Lily has become a bit fussy with her food of late. Her former love of healthier snacks like hummus and carrots or pitta bread has faded. She is still claiming to be a vegetarian, but I have my doubts after finding the packaging of a chicken sandwich in her school bag. I saw it and left it in there. She'll work things out in her own time. Lloyd and I genuinely feel like we're her mum and dad after all this time. She is absolutely part of our family, though lately some issues have been raising themselves.

'So, I'm hearing yes, yes, yes with conditions, and – Lloyd?'

'If I say yes, can I go and watch another episode of the *Star Wars* thing?'

He's been totally hooked on a series about the history of how they made Star Wars. I must admit I've sat down and watched a few episodes because the story of how they went from cardboard and sticky tape to sophisticated technology is genuinely amazing. When Lloyd's excited about a new series or book he's pretty much agreeable to most things.

Everyone else seems indifferent. They're so used to foster siblings by now, it's just not a big deal. We appear to have 'given it some thought' and my take away from the brief dinner conversation is a 'yes' to looking into welcoming a new child.

'Excellent. That's settled then. I shall get on to Kendi.'

Kendi is our new supervising social worker. He did his training on the East coast of Africa, and came to England to do his Masters in human rights law. I'm rather fond of him, as is Lloyd. He brings a certain level of joy to our work as he has a way about him that is both endearing and carries gravitas, an unusual blend. He also has a wonderfully expressive face that reveals all his thoughts. I've advised him never to play poker…

But there's something else to deal with first.

'Andrea says I can have open phone contact with Mum!'

'Does she, indeed?'

I'm getting rather frustrated with what 'Andrea says'.

Andrea is Lily's new social worker, and we're hearing 'Andrea says' rather more than I'd like since she started. Most of the time I like her, even though she's always running late and perpetually yawning. She's a real local. A woman who grew up in the area, who went to the local school and whose parents still live two roads away from us. She has three children of her own and a husband who works for a skip-hire company. I only know this because we were forced to hire a skip last winter when a part of our stone wall fell down after heavy snow.

'Oh, that's one of my husband's!' Andrea said, beaming when she saw it on the street outside our house on one of her visits. She was inordinately chuffed that we were using one of her husband's skips.

I also like her because she had an interesting route into social work. She used to be a children's escort for a taxi firm that was being run by a friend of hers. They got a contract to drive lots of CLAs (Child Looked After) as they were known, to school. Now they're called 'Children We Care For' or CWCFs. And before they were CLAs they were LACs (Looked After Child). I don't know why they keep changing the name. But I digress. Getting to know those children and their stories on the school run each day influenced Andrea to retrain as a social worker. She's a very kind person, and I think social work appeals to that innate kindness. Fresh-faced and earnest, she gives 'Mother Earth' vibes.

She's very *nice*, but also one of those people who you feel never quite thinks things through and, so far, has made some significant decisions for Lily that haven't included us. As her foster carers for so long, this feels uncomfortable.

And this is one of them.

'So, I've been texting Mum this afternoon.' Lily lays it down as a challenge.

To agree to contact with Lily's birth mother, open phone contact, without any discussion with us, isn't on. On the surface it might sound as if there's nothing wrong with it. Why shouldn't Lily have contact with her own mother? But this is the very same person whom authorities decided wasn't safe for the children to be with. The same person for whom contact workers were required to be present during contact.

And this isn't the first time it's happened with a foster child. With multiple text messaging platforms and FaceTime, parents now have instant, unsupervised access to their children, even after a judge has decided that they shouldn't. It's a thorny issue. Why remove them from the abuse and neglect by putting them in care, only to give the source of the abuse a way back into their lives?

'Bloody mobile phones,' I think and then realise I must've muttered it out loud when Lily says, 'What?!'

'I was just thinking about mobile phones, generally,' I manage to recover.

They really are the bane of my fostering life. We've had a series of serious problems with different foster children of late, the root cause of which has been mobile phones. Sky, Sparkle and Willow were all children who stayed with us and were undone by them in different ways.

After dinner I raise the issue on the foster carers' WhatsApp group.

Funnily enough, Lily is not the only young teenage foster child to have been encouraged to have open contact with their birth mum and other family members.

The reason I'm so cross about it in Lily's case is because, for the first time since she arrived with us, we're beginning to struggle with Lily's behaviour and the pushing of boundaries. With constant access to her birth mum, our relationship will change even more, I'm sure of it.

This discussion quickly escalates into an unprovoked, 'I hate you,' and Lily disappearing upstairs. Part of me wonders if she is also 'grieving' after losing her long-standing social worker.

The previous one was in her life for more than five years, but left recently to go overseas because her husband is an army officer and was posted to support UN peacekeeping missions in Africa.

We adored her; she was a lovely person and Lily trusted her. She would not have let this 24/7 phone contact situation happen, or at least not without clear boundaries in place and an agreement between us all.

In the morning I contact Kendi, not just to tell him that we'll look at referrals for placements, but to update him on the latest Lily development.

He's not impressed with Andrea's actions either.

He makes a low whistling sound that clearly signals his disapproval. I can't see his face on the phone but I imagine that he's shaking his head and puffing out his cheeks as he says, 'I don't understand why this country cannot make a law to protect children from the dangers of their phones.'

'I know!'

'It is the toothless animal that arrives first at the base of the tree, to eat his fill before the others arrive.' He has a way with words that I love but can't always follow. He's a very honest, religious person, though he never talks about his faith other than by referencing other parishioners. 'I know a wonderful man from my church who…' or, 'there is a very clever woman from my church that…' I like to think of his church as a great big, spiritual HR department.

'I also wanted to discuss the idea of us putting our hat back in the ring for another placement. We all discussed it at dinner last night, and we think it's time.'

He doesn't need to know that 'discussed' is a bit strong to describe the fairly superficial level of conversation that took place.

'How long is it since you said goodbye to Willow?'

'We've reached the six-month mark now.'

'Hmmm.' It was Kendi who suggested that we have

the six month break given the circumstances of Willow's departure and the sadness we all felt.

'I feel like we could do with a distraction: a new placement, a new child and a new challenge. It might help to take my mind off things.'

'Like Lily?'

'Not just that. I love the excitement that every placement brings.'

I tell him about Lily's reluctance to have another girl in the house.

'So a boy, then?'

'Yes, a younger boy. Still in primary school. That will be a good match, I think.'

'It will be interesting, after teenagers.'

'I know!'

Now that I have the idea of a younger boy fixed in my brain I start to sort out the spare room ready for occupancy once again. There are so many children waiting for placements that it won't be long before one arrives with us. I think back to what Jackson and Vincent liked when they were younger and how they wanted their rooms to be. We've looked after boys before and, my word, some of them had heartbreaking stories to tell, though I don't want to pre-empt anything. We never know what a child will be like and I have to remember that, just because he is a boy, it doesn't automatically mean he'll want to kick a ball around with Lloyd.

Actually, scrub that. I've never actually seen Lloyd kick

a ball. It was me who took the boys to the park to play football and a version of cricket. (That's probably why they don't shine in the sports department.) I always imagined I'd have two strapping lads doing rugby or football, but neither Jackson nor Vincent have shown too much enthusiasm. And Lily was more interested in dance. She's been to the local studio for a lesson and is thinking about signing up for classes. I was keen to make sure that she absolutely *does* want to do it before I fork out for all the gear.

I walk out and head to my 'cupboard of dreams', or the linen cupboard as it's known to most people. I'll begin thinking about bedding for a potential arrival. Stuffed with hand soap, there's always a delightful, concentrated aroma hit when I open the door. I like to pull both doors open simultaneously with my eyes closed, ready to inhale the heady fragrances. Wonderful. Deep breath. Inspiration. Deep breath. Peace.

But after the soap scent-hit, I open my eyes and see — well — a *violation* of my life. Order no longer reigns! They've left towels half-cock, hanging down from shelves, some dropped at the bottom of the cupboard. 'They' being the kids. It's a total mess. They used to have one towel at a time each, colour-coded so that we all knew which towel belonged to which child. For some reason they've all now taken to having three each. One for their body, one for their hair and separate face towels. Then they chuck them on the washing pile every day. Little do they know that I don't actually wash them daily. I pick them up, hang them out to air and dry and they are none the wiser. Imagine having to wash nine towels every day. This isn't a hotel, and none of them have health issues that require such frequent washing – so no, thank you!

When I go back to my computer, trying not to fume about having had to refold towels, I see that Kendi has sent over two referrals. Both for older children. I just don't think that will work with the current dynamic and Lily's building behaviour and attitude. I'm going to be firm about this.

Looking at the referrals, it strikes me that they'd both need so much attention. It would take me away from the others too much. It's harder when they're all the same age. They notice everything; how much time, money and energy I give to each one. There's some sort of mental spreadsheet they have, calculating what's fair.

Jackson and Vincent have always been very generous and not in any sense needy, but they're very aware when things become unbalanced and they need to know that we're here for them, too. No. We'll just wait until the right child comes along.

It takes far longer than I expect it to. There are some girls who we turn down, mainly because of Lily, and more older children. But I've given so much in the past and I've taken in children against my better judgement so I stick to my guns. Several weeks pass before we receive a referral for a boy, aged seven years, called Milo.

II

I sit in the back garden with a coffee, reading over Milo's referral. Jackahuahua dogs are small, but I have *both* Dotty and Douglas settled on my lap, and Mabel, Lily's cat, is trying to squeeze in and find a place too. It's a pleasantly warm day for the summer we've had so far. It seems to oscillate between singeingly hot and dull grey at the moment, with nothing very much in between. I can't seem to get the clothes right. I'm hot, then cold. I don't know if it's the climate crisis, or just me in the throes of the menopause. Bring it on, frankly. The menopause, that is. I'm looking forward to the years of being rewarded by not having periods.

I look down at the text once again. I have to read referrals several times to try to decode them. I'm not sure that, in my whole fostering career, I've ever received a referral that genuinely reflected the child who walked through our door. They can be awful attempts at marketing a child, pushing the truth as close to a lie as they can – or beyond. I've giggled as I have read some. Once I laughed out loud because, by some sort of administrative mistake, I received the referral for a child we'd already fostered and said goodbye to. Now, that was a comedy masterpiece. Lloyd and I sat in the kitchen in disbelief as the referral, aimed at parking this child as soon as possible, glossed over all the elements of need. It was truly astonishing.

But this referral doesn't even have his date of birth. It has a former address for him in an area that I've visited before: front doors hanging off, washing machines and fridges in front gardens. It's a place that I discovered while dropping off a teenage foster child to her friend's house. We'd been working with a rather tricky social worker who'd been critical of me, and of our home. She described it as 'chaotic' and, bizarrely, as being 'too colourful'.

I wonder how Farrow and Ball would feel about that, seeing as most of our home is painted with their shades. While I sat in the car texting Lloyd about picking up some spices for our curry for dinner, I looked up and couldn't believe what I saw. Coming out of one of the shabby houses, where the grass in the front garden had grown the height of the gate (and not in a no-mow May, be friendly to the insects way, or at least not as the plentiful pile of rusting appliances in the front garden would suggest), this same social worker was putting her rubbish in her bin.

The opportunity was too good to resist.

While she was fiddling about with the bins, dressed in her giant claw slippers, (and quite what a grown woman is doing with ridiculous, novelty fur-fabric feet is anybody's guess), I opened my car door and got out of the car. I waved cheerfully, calling out to her and making sure that she looked up and saw me. She wasn't quite so nasty after that.

Still, it's the same estate that Milo was living on.

In the next sentence, Milo is described as *a loving child*.

That sends me through the roof. Firstly, how would the social worker actually know that? By which I mean what does being 'loving' mean, and what does it look like? I am far happier watching children display healthy caution around adults, rather than being touchy-feely and clingy. So the first alarm bell has been set off, clanging loudly in the peace of my garden. Reading between the lines, perhaps I'm in fact reading about a boy who may potentially have attachment issues. He may have been abused and exploited.

Milo is next described as *lively and full of beans*. Oh yes, I know this one very well. What this means is that Milo, as with so many children who come into care, has not experienced safe boundaries. He'll have some sort of behaviour issues that are usually not their fault, instead the result of a distinct lack of good parenting.

Sometimes it's a lack of *any* parenting. Another reason that a child might have behaviour issues, and sadly one that I've also encountered too many times, arises from foetal alcohol spectrum disorder (FASD) where they have been subject to drug and alcohol damage pre-birth. But it might also be connected to ADHD (Attention Deficit Hyperactivity

Disorder). And the trouble is that not enough doctors know the difference between the two which leads to the danger of misdiagnosis. It might look, statistically, as if there are a greater number of children with ADHD living in poverty when in fact ADHD is classless. The behaviours of ADHD are similar to drug and alcohol damage. The difference is that ADHD is a neurodevelopmental condition. Those with ADHD experience the world differently because of their neuro wiring. Drug and alcohol damage is exactly that: damage, and requires a very different approach.

So, two sets of alarms are now ringing.

Experience tells me what all this means.

It means that anything and everything could happen with this young fella.

I shake my head and move on. I can't take too unpredictable right now. I slide the various animals down from my lap now that I'm down to the last dregs of my coffee cup. The children are sorted, the tomatoes are watered (along with the lavender trees in pots that seem to be permanently dry), and time is marching on. I look down and realise that I'm still in my pyjamas! There is much to do, as always. I have to write my logs to put on 'Charms', the current system that we upload our weekly logs onto. I certainly don't find it charming. I'm a bad student and sometimes it's every two weeks, not always on a Sunday evening as I think we agreed with Kendi at the start. But, hey ho, life is never the same two weeks in a row, and I have always lived the sort of life that refuses to run to a particular schedule. I know Kendi understands. He always says, 'I know you will get the logs there when you have time.'

First, a shower. After which it's time to do a sweep of the children's rooms for rubbish, laundry and anything that probably should require a white hazmat suit.

I try to put young Milo out of my mind.

III

But Milo has other ideas. Or at least the referral team do. His referral lands in my inbox for a second time a couple of days later. I know that we felt we couldn't take on anyone too unpredictable right now, but the fact is, every foster placement is unpredictable. People are unpredictable. Children are unpredictable.

There is a shortage of foster carers everywhere, hence the rise in independent fostering agencies. At the last count, nearly 20,000 households in the UK have taken in children via this route. There are too many children in the system – more than 100,000 of them, and not enough resources to go round.

I spent a long time looking at Milo's referral and he's got into my head.

I'm also conscious that, because we have a lot of experience behind us now, we might be better placed than some to help. When we welcomed our first *wild child* into our house we were, frankly, winging it, despite the training. The training actually hardly touches the sides of what a foster carer needs to know in the face of the realities of fostering.

Hmm. Milo, Milo, Milo. I refer to my research assistant, otherwise known as Google. The name Milo means 'soldier'. I wonder how much battling this one's had to do in his life so far. Too much, by the sound of things. I still have the referral details printed off on my desk.

I sigh, pick them up, and pop into Lloyd's office to see what he thinks about Milo.

He smiles. 'I see they're still playing with language and pretending that there's nothing to see here!'

I laugh. 'Yes, Lloyd. I reckon we can play the usual game of 'opposites' on this one.' It's a regular and usually valid practice to assume that a referral means more or less the opposite of what it actually says. It's a bit like fostering and social work more widely. If we were just told the truth from the outset, it wouldn't stop the right people from applying, but it might prevent some of the frustration and disappointment once they'd entered those careers.

'So… is that a yes?'

He shrugs.

I shake the A4 pages of the referral triumphantly at my audience (the dogs). 'I'll let Kendi know,' I tell them.

My email is soon sent, which means that wheels will be in motion. Kendi will need to speak with Lily's social worker before anything else can happen, so we'll be waiting on Andrea to respond.

There's nothing else to do in the meantime but wait. The waiting game always feels weird. Once you start to imagine a child, you become invested in that individual. While the wait goes on, you feel an element of anxiety that you may not get the child that you have agreed to welcome into your home. Something will happen to interfere. Human beings are predictably unpredictable.

I know that it's usually a waste of time and money to fill out a room for a child you haven't met yet. It can create tensions too. They may feel pressured to express a like for things that they actually don't. What I have carefully curated for them might not be what they want. We can feel disappointed and, perhaps worst of all, start to feel that they are ungrateful for what we've done. But that's ridiculous, because how can they be ungrateful for something they had no knowledge of ever wanting?

So, instead of arranging the bedroom, I sort out the garden. The wet weather in between the hot spells has meant that the weeds have flourished and the slugs and snails have feasted on many of my plants. The poor dahlias didn't stand a chance. For once I get up to date with all my work and then I get a call from Andrea.

'Hi, Louise. Just wanted to feedback Lily's mum's views on you having a new placement.'

I'm stunned, my thoughts running along the lines of: *what the actual f**k?*

Andrea ran our new placement idea past *Lily's mum?*

I focus and my eyes narrow to the point where I can hardly see anything. I let her talk.

'The good news is that she's okay with it in principle, but she has some questions, so if we can just discuss those?'

Right, I have heard enough.

'Andrea, with respect, a new placement, our home, our lives is of no business to Lily's mum.' I am seething. 'May I ask you what your rationale was in speaking to Lily's mum about something that has absolutely nothing to do with her?'

To my surprise, she says, 'Well, Louise, it does actually, since her daughter lives with you.'

I am steaming.

Lloyd suddenly appears at the door, obviously curious to find out what's causing the acid tone of my voice. I make the big eyes and pursed lip face that he knows means *I'm talking to an idiot*. He's seen me do it plenty of times before, most recently when a racist was having a go at a child because their ball had gone into the road. Suddenly that ball became a symbol for the whole of the national debt because it was being chased by a boy whose mother was black. I laid into him in a way that he could not respond to because, like all bigots, they have limitations which become apparent fairly quickly.

I decide that as soon as this phone call is over, I am contacting Kendi, and then I will make a formal complaint. If nothing else, then GDPR, the General Data Protection Regulation laws must come into play here. The fostering services have access to our personal data but that doesn't mean they can share it. Surely we have a right to privacy?

I put in the complaint, formally, in writing. I know that there will be repercussions but Andrea's attitude has made me so angry and, frankly, I'm long past going to the effort of second-guessing what these people may or may not do. Bring it on!

When I speak to Kendi I can hear the usual smile and warmth in his voice when he says, straight away, 'No, no, you are right, she should not have done that.'

But he also reveals that, despite Andrea's interfering actions, she has said 'yes' to the suggested placement. We will continue with the referral for Milo.

I'm thrilled. It feels like a little mini victory amidst the sometimes weird decision-making of children's social care. Onwards to find out more about Milo.

'I'll arrange a Teams call between you and the department manager because, at the present moment, Milo is without a social worker,' Kendi promises.

That news is unsurprising. Social workers are, like foster carers, becoming pretty thin on the ground. I'm pleased about the Teams meeting and, as always, feel looked after by Kendi. He has our backs. It's a situation that should be normal, for your supervising social worker to have your back, but we had to actively seek it out by moving from the local authority to an independent fostering agency.

Kendi, in his typically efficient way, sets the Teams video

meeting for the following day. It goes well and the manager seems nice enough, but I can tell that she is distracted while we're talking. She keeps looking at the messages interrupting her screen and her speech slows down while she's obviously thinking about something else. I like the backdrops the social workers use when they are in the car, office or, more commonly, working from home. I find the Dubai-style hotel lobbies or tropical gardens amusing when they're in a hot sweaty car with their windows closed so passersby can't hear the conversation.

This manager has a beach backdrop but I have a distinct feeling that she's in a car somewhere in a car park. And why not? As time goes on, I feel more and more compassion for social workers and the job that they have to do in the trying circumstances of large caseloads and historic underfunding. Always one hand tied behind their backs. Though I'm less charitable when loose cannons like Andrea make insane judgements.

It is quickly agreed that Milo will arrive this Friday – three days' time – giving us the weekend to get to know him before he starts his new school on Monday. He has a place at a relatively new school in the next county which, in reality, is closer to our front door than popping to the big Sainsbury's in town because we live so close to the border. The referral does state a few items of food that Milo has a preference for. No surprises there: chips, chicken nuggets and ice cream. I feel a trip to the big Sainsbury's coming on.

We must get everything ready for young Milo. I'm excited, as are the others. Even Lily lightens her mood a little and asks questions about him.

'Go on then, tell us what you know.'

When I explain where he lives, Lily makes a funny voice. 'Road man!' The way she says it makes it sound like 'wrowed mun'.

I still don't fully understand what they mean when they say 'road man', except that it is derogatory and suggests a certain look and a certain streetwise attitude, and probably a drug gang connection. 'First of all, he's seven, right? And anyway, just because he comes from a certain postcode doesn't make him a road man. I expect that some are Emos just like you.'

She scoffs at that. 'I'm not an Emo, I'm a Vinted Vigilante.'

I look confused, because I am. She, like the boys, has discovered Vinted, the online marketplace that enables teenagers to cultivate a secondhand wardrobe that might otherwise be way beyond their means. It's Millie's fault, Lloyd's daughter. In her early 30s, she's very hip, very beautiful and very much a role model. And she loves Vinted. Lloyd now also likes Vinted because he's made it his job to go to the Spar or Tesco's to post their packages through a funny door. He seems to love it. I have no idea how it all works. I'm just happy that Lily is smiling and chatting.

But not for long. Lily has dance after school, and only

now presents me with her sweaty dance gear. I must have dreamt that I'd already washed it.

'I don't have a magic wand, you know.'

'But it's gross! I can't wear it like that.'

The tone is accusatory, the implication that it's my fault.

'Give it here,' I concede. 'I'll see what I can do.'

After their departures, I head for the dog leads hanging up in the kitchen. Cue two very excited pooches in anticipation of their walkies. My mobile rings. It's the social work manager asking if we can take Milo today.

'Ideally by lunch time. His current foster carer has had a family crisis and needs him out today.'

IV

Part of the work we do as foster carers relies on the ability to be flexible and respond calmly to a crisis. Which is why we should be considered the fourth emergency service.

I wish I was that cool. Instead, I'm thrown into a tizzy. I feel angry, disorientated and generally rubbish. But I quickly dismiss those childish thoughts and tell myself, 'You've got this!'

I go into Lloyd's office where I find him busy talking to Sharon, a lovely client of many years. I whisper, 'Change of plan. Milo is coming this lunch time.' I shrug my shoulders at his raised eyebrow and head out of the door with the dogs. I do the walk around the field so fast it's almost a run. Good job no one was there to see or they might have thought I was dying. I drag myself back home and guzzle a pint of water in about two seconds. Dogs done. Next! I should have a bell to ding as I smash my way through each task.

I zoom to the supermarket and buy the usual, covering all food bases: oven chips, chicken nuggets, hash browns, pizzas, burgers – beef and vegetarian – and white bread. My children, especially Vincent, now like good sourdough or brown nutty bread. But most of the children I've met who come into foster care would rather have some plain white bread. And, to be fair, old-school bacon sandwiches are much better with white bread, so I'm not complaining.

Now that the initial 'fear' has passed, I'm moving straight into 'thrive' mode. As I've got older I've learnt that my initial panic reaction to these sorts of situations is driven by my human need to survive. The ancient brain that sits at the back of our heads works on intuition. When predators were around we learnt to panic to be safe. Now I panic because I haven't made a bed. Different era, different danger. Predators! I'll get the t-rex duvet set from my airing cupboard of scented joy. I dash back home, unpack the shopping, and I'm just smoothing down the changed bed when I realise that any minute now Milo will be here – and Kendi isn't.

Shit.

Of course he isn't. I haven't even spoken to him about the change of plan. I text him with lightning speed on my way down the stairs.

Milo is coming NOW.

I can see that 'Kendi is typing' then see *What, are you okay? I'll be there as soon as I can. I'm with another foster family on the other side of the county.*

I know him and I know he will honour his word. I just hope he doesn't get a speeding ticket. The traffic police are out and about. They got me two weeks ago as I was coming back into town. I was driving down a hill in a small village that has a swooping turn. It got me. I was going 36mph in a 30 limit. It was nearly 8pm. I didn't expect a police traffic controller person with a hand-held camera in the bushes. I was in the wrong, and that's that.

In a way, I think parenting should be treated like using the roads. Here are the laws, here is the guidance. If you break the law and there's evidence to prove it, then tough. You get a speeding conviction. You can reduce your sentence if you do the course. Your punishment is two weeks without Ben and Jerry's and wine. There, that would do it. Or two weeks without a break from your family. Ha! No extenuating circumstances. Even more of an incentive. Parenting is the new driving. Just put me in charge of dishing out the convictions. Oh dear, now I actually feel dizzy. I'm feeling galvanised by speeding tickets. I have completely wound myself up and I'm wasting precious energy in idle fantasy. I hate the idea that I am not prepared for a new arrival.

I hate it because it means that the child coming into our home may not feel welcome. And that is something I pride myself on. It's the most frequent thing I hear from children we've fostered: the feeling that they are welcomed.

When I was a child, being 'welcomed' was not a feeling that I had any option to think about. The fact that now children can express how they feel is crucial for us in knowing how best to help them. With children who come into care, it's often all about the small stuff. So much is messed up in their wider world that the little details are important. Like that wonderful saying, *if you look after your pennies, the pounds will look after themselves.* Sometimes, with children in care, it's all about the nuances: the smells, the feelings, the atmosphere. Children who have experienced abuse and neglect have a heightened sense of these things. They will read your face in a nanosecond to see if they will be safe or not.

I still do it, and my own care days are a long time ago now. Nevertheless, I'm programmed to read people very quickly and, now that I am a confident capable adult, I no longer read the faces of others just to decide if I'm safe, I read them to decide if I can help.

So, I push thoughts of speeding tickets away and take a deep breath as I loiter in the vacuum of time before I hear the doorbell. It's not enough time to do anything, just fiddle about annoying Lloyd as he tries to rattle off a job so he can help with the meet and greet of Milo.

Then, there it is. Not the doorbell, but a little tap tap tap on the glass. A timid sound, not the usual bailiff's knock that the postman makes, or the impatient one of a child who has forgotten their key. This is the knock of a meek and tentative person.

I usher Dotty and Douglas into the hall and shut the door. This knock does not fill me with confidence. I head to the door and open it wide, to see a small boy with blonde hair swaying from side to side and a young woman, not much taller than the boy. What a funny looking pair. *Phineas and Ferb* spring to mind, but it's too weird to make the connection with cartoon animations so I reject it and invite them in.

'Hello! Hello! Come in! This way. Come on through.'

I watch this strange duo enter our lives. Milo is like an alert sparrow, watching everything as we go towards the kitchen. She, I don't yet know her name because she hasn't offered it, is like a character from a Beatrix Potter book. There is something of Mrs Tiggywinkle about her. She is wearing a dark brown small flower print dress . It has a white cotton collar and looks like something from Laura Ashley in the 70s. No one has introduced themselves. It's all a bit odd. I decide to put that right once we meet Doug and Dotty. I look at Milo and say, 'Hello Milo, I'm Louise and this is Douglas and Dotty. I look at Mrs Tiggywinkle and, as if she has only just remembered it's a good idea, she smiles.

'Hello, I'm Daisy.'

Lloyd comes in and smiles. He puts his hand out to Daisy, who looks terrified.

I say, 'Lloyd, this is Milo,' and point at the boy who is now on his knees playing with the dogs. This is a good sign. If a child is at ease with my foster doggies they will be able to do a lot of 'good therapeutic work'. Well, that's my experience, and what I tell anyone else from the care system. It's a bit like 'art therapy'. Somehow, doing really normal stuff like playing with animals or drawing and making things has been made into a therapeutic activity. This is a great shame because it means that now these normal things tend to have an element of assessment or measurement involved with them.

My fellow fostering friend, Christine, still laughs about the visit she had from a social worker who praised her for her deep therapeutic work in enabling the children in her care to make a safe space to think. Basically, it was a lovely day and Christine wanted the children outside and out from under her feet. She gave them a load of old sheets to make a good, old-fashioned den.

I sometimes think that children's social care is a bit like the art world. It's subjective and occasionally uses language in a high-falutin way. Pompous, or as I might be tempted to describe it, 'bullshit', which somehow adds value to the art. Maybe this level of therapeutic overlay adds value to the professionals who enjoy talking about it. Who knows? But Milo is happy with the pooches and that's great!

'So, Daisy, would you like a cup of tea?'

'Have you got any herbal tea?' she asks, very quietly.

I note Lloyd's face. He looks like he's doing an impression of an ocker 1970s' Australian, manfully cooking his meat on a BBQ who's just been asked if he could cook a veggie bean burger.

Before he has a chance to say anything untoward, I leap in. 'Yes, of course. We have mint, green tea, or some camomile, I think.'

She rootles around in her bag and then proffers a tea bag. 'It's okay, I carry my own.'

Fine. At least she hasn't offered up her own mug which has happened before and I can't help but find insulting. It's a gesture usually followed with, 'I always provide my own cup as so many houses are so dirty you have to wipe your feet on the way out.'

Daisy watches Milo like a hawk. She looks nervous. I'm a seasoned foster carer, more than capable of reading a situation like this and carefully tuned-in to non-verbal cues. What is she worried about?

I learn that she is not Milo's actual social worker. His social worker, who is a locum, is away on leave. That could well be code for 'gone'. She is only here today, she explains, because the situation was an emergency.

'The foster carer, Michelle, had a family crisis and couldn't take Milo with her.'

Hmm. Again, I'm too long in the tooth to accept this level of flannel.

I place Daisy's cup in front of her and decide, rather childishly perhaps, not to offer her a biscuit. I walk towards Milo who is now lying down on the floor in the hallway being kissed by Douglas and laughing his head off.

'Milo, would you like a drink and a snack?'

He pays no attention, too busy enjoying Doug's therapeutic input.

Lloyd is already sitting down with a black coffee and a face full of disdain. I can tell he's not bowled over by Daisy's demeanour. Time for a bit of ice-breaking.

'So Daisy, how long have you been a social worker?'

She looks a little put out by the question.

'I'm on work placement. It's my second year at uni,' she admits, uneasily.

Oh, I think. I now know that she will have a bit of theoretical knowledge and no experience. It rather suggests she has been dropped in it. That's not fair. I feel a little bit more compassion for her. I see and hear about this happening more and more as students are being used for frontline work because there's a national shortage of social workers as well as a crisis in the numbers of foster carers leaving.

My initial annoyance at her lack of confidence shifts to feelings of sympathy and, if I'm honest, a little concern. I suspect she doesn't know terribly much about how a placement meeting goes.

Suddenly, Milo jumps up from the floor and darts out of the room.

'Milo, do you want me to show you…' I trail off, because obviously he doesn't want me to show him anything. He careers out into the hallway, swiping everything that's on the console table onto the floor as he goes. My lipstick, that I keep tucked behind a small plant, ready for emergency reapplications, clatters to the floor, as does the small plant. The pot shatters to smithereens on the flagstones and I hear Milo thundering up the stairs. He makes a surprisingly loud thump for such a slight boy.

'Never liked that pot anyway,' I say brightly as I return

to the kitchen and grab the dustpan and brush to begin sweeping up the debris. The lipstick appears to have survived.

A few seconds later Milo races back down the stairs. He's like the Road Runner character in the cartoon. I almost expect to hear a 'beep-beep' from him and see smoke at his heels, Wile E. Coyote in hot pursuit.

He shoots through the kitchen and out into the back garden. The weather is fine today so we've left the back door open. I've already done a poop swoop so it's safe to run around out there. Daisy looks a little frightened by the havoc and chaos of the last 30 seconds. She stands up and moves towards the kitchen window. I stand next to her and watch Milo fly around the garden. Is he pretending to be an aeroplane? His arms are out and he's running fast, as if he wants to take off.

Daisy knocks on the window and calls to Milo, 'Time to come in.'

Well, it's not, I think to myself. It's time to run your little legs off in the garden and get some fresh air. And there's less to crash into out there. He looks pasty, like he has been kept indoors. All foster children, no matter what age or size, seem to want to go out and feel the wind in their hair if they have been feeling cooped up. I love watching children run free, but his excitement is worrying her. I can see he has a wildness about him, but why is it worrying her so much?

I ask her another question. 'Daisy, how long have you known Milo?'

She makes a strange sound, part way between a cough and a throat-clear. 'Oh, only recently.'

I dig a bit deeper. 'How long ago is recently?'

She looks out of the window again. 'Today.'

I let out a low whistle, but give Daisy a reassuring smile.

I ask Lloyd to keep window-watch. 'Shall we sit down?' I ask Daisy, knowing that I need to try to figure out what is actually going on.

Daisy sits down, gathering her skirts around her like a character from a different age. She's young. More than a decade younger than my youngest step-daughter, Millie.

I cut to the chase. 'Daisy, do you have particular concerns about Milo?'

She looks very uncomfortable. I know that her line manager's manager will have made it very clear to her that she basically needs to park Milo today. If that means not telling the whole story, so be it. But that's not going to help any of us.

'Daisy, is there something that you think we should know but have been instructed not to tell us?'

She looks like she might be about to speak, but her face is forlorn.

This is not fair. She is so inexperienced and out of her depth.

Suddenly the door goes. 'Kendi!' I leap up and head straight to open the door wide. 'Good to see you,' I say, nice and loud. Then I whisper. 'We have a wild boy and a very naïve social worker. I'm fairly certain she's keeping something from us.'

Kendi looks at me and smiles. 'No problem.' Even just by being here he makes everything feel a little bit better. He walks smartly into the kitchen with his briefcase. He must be the only person I know who carries a briefcase. I wonder if it's because of the TV he grew-up with. I love it. He's such a mix of so many things, and you never know quite which one you're going to get. But it's always the right one.

Now he is like the 'Man from the Ministry'. He sits down opposite Daisy and beams at her. I think for a moment that he's going to say that he's here to represent his clients, Louise and Lloyd. Instead, the dulcet tones merely say, 'Hello, Daisy. I am Kendi. I am Louise and Lloyd's supervising social worker.'

I make him a cup of tea with five sugars. I raised my eyebrows the first time, but I've got used to the fact that he always has five. From his briefcase he pulls out a few bits of paperwork. I don't know how he's got that already. He must have gone back to the office before he came to us. Good lord, this man is a ninja James Bond. Daisy frowns and bites her bottom lip, looking decidedly perplexed.

Lloyd is creeping out towards the back garden, which indicates that he has a few concerns. I stand up and look out of the window. Ah. The tomato plants are no longer upright. The pots are on their sides. Lloyd reaches them and stands them back up. Although they're in big plastic pots they dry out very easily, so they're easy to push over. The wind does it too.

I watch as Lloyd heads off down the garden to persuade Milo not to pull over my big stone heads that I'm rather fond of. He appears to be winning although I can't hear the details of the conversation. It looks as though he's offering to show Milo the garden toy box.

I'm trying to focus on two things at once, because I'm also listening to Kendi ask Daisy what the real reason is for Milo's sudden arrival.

'Michelle, uh, had a family crisis. That's it. A family crisis.'

She repeats those words again, and Kendi decides not to pursue it. I think he wants her to know that he – we – are not wet behind the ears. He manages to look stern and kind at the same time. I think he hopes this intel will get back to her line managers.

But I already feel worried. I don't want to upset another feisty manager by raising concerns. I'm well aware that there have been times in the past where I have hit a nerve and know that I can then look forward to an allegation, or complaint at the least. It can feel like working with the Stasi. I try not to get paranoid just yet. Milo hasn't even been here an hour, but I have become wary. I don't want Kendi to push it any more.

Paperwork is swapped and signed and I ask about Delegated Authority – the legal process that gives me leeway to make common sense decisions on behalf of a child *in loco parentis*. It covers very ordinary things that you wouldn't otherwise think twice about: signing consent forms for school trips or allowing him to go to a friend's house for a sleepover. I need to feel that I can make decisions about those sorts of things, and take him to the doctors' surgery, optician and dentist – if we can find one. That seems straightforward enough.

I ask about contact with his family. Again, it's good to know upfront what the situation is likely to be, but I'm also, as always, aiming to try to eke out more information about Milo's family background. I learn nothing more than that contact arrangements will be made after he has settled in. Daisy appears to be feeling a little more relaxed than when she first tiptoed through the door. Perhaps she feels less threatened now, and more as if we are on the same side rather than in conflict. It's Kendi who has worked his magic, tactfully asking about her studentship a few times.

'What subject have you decided to focus on for your thesis, Daisy?'

She explains that she has chosen to explore the concept of 'good enough parenting'. I'm pretty sure that one has been covered by a few social work students but Kendi praises the choice and offers her some reading suggestions. I honestly believe he could smooth out any situation. He should be employed by the UN rather than the local social services team.

I see something out of the corner of my eye. It's a basket, flying past the window. I wonder how that's happened? Lloyd is perfectly capable of managing a young boy in the back garden, surely?

'So, do you have Milo's bags, Daisy?' I ask, trying to ignore whatever is happening beyond the window.

'I'll go and get it from the car.'

I walk through the hall with her. Heightwise, she just about comes to my shoulder and I wonder how she will cope when working with teenagers. A small stature to go with that shrinking nature isn't the most commanding combination. She goes out to her old burgundy Fiat Punto and brings in a large plastic shopping bag, the sort you can get by the checkout at TKMaxx. I watch her drive away and notice the green 'just passed' P on the back of her car. I take a quick peep in the bag and see one fluffy toy, a handful of clothes and a clear plastic bag with a toothbrush.

That's it.

I pull the blue toy out, which looks like a koala gone wrong, and realise it's Disney's Stitch, from the *Lilo & Stitch* franchise, a genetically engineered, extraterrestrial life-form also known as Experiment 626. It seems apt. Given what little knowledge his training-to-be-a-social-worker chaperone has, Milo might himself be experiment number goodness-knows-what in the care system.

I head back into the kitchen.

'She's gone?' Kendi observes with a frown. 'I thought she was just going to get his bag.'

So did I, now I come to think of it. It is rather odd, too,

that she hasn't even said goodbye to Milo – nor Lloyd or Kendi for that matter.

I look out of the window. Lloyd is still out in the garden with Milo. It looks as if he is attempting to teach him bouncing and catching skills. Milo is laughing, which is a good sign. But the laugh has taken over his whole body, so that it looks as if he's shaking at the same time. He's a funny little fella and, as so often with new arrivals, one of my first thoughts is that he looks like he needs feeding up. Poor chap, he has a sweet face but there is something vacant about it at the same time. Like he's not fully engaged with his surroundings.

I watch more closely, making further visual assessments of him. He holds his hands balled up very tightly. It's early days, but I'm already beginning to wonder if we are looking at another child with Foetal Alcohol Damage. There have been a few of those over the years. If that's the case, then – well, we're in difficult territory.

I feel myself bracing for a rollercoaster ride. Thoughts whorl around inside the vortex of my mind. It will mean having to battle for every little penny and service available from the local authority, as they face a growing demand in this area. The figures are on the rise. More mothers seem to drink and take drugs during pregnancy. That is not to apportion blame. So many do not even know that they are pregnant. There is increasing awareness that girls are having sex without even understanding how their periods work. Or they may have been abused or raped. It's an endless, dystopic downwards slope as we see children born, through no fault of their own, with these disorders and damage. There is no money. One in 10 local authorities are going bankrupt. The staff will be briefed to avoid expenditure as much as they can, while the strategic communication and public image promotes the idea that these organisations care.

I am having a 'foster carer's clarity attack'. They happen more and more often these days. It's automatic. The sharpening of the mind, the quick, strategy-development work needed to adjust our lives to support this young person who has been dropped into our home. We can't give him back now that we've tried him out for an hour or two.

Milo deserves his chance, whatever his story. Every child does.

Nevertheless, I feel as if I am already getting the gist of his story – and I don't like it.

As if reading my thoughts, Kendi stands up and joins me at the window. 'You're going to have your hands full with this one, Louise.'

'Are you up for the fight, Kendi?' I turn to look at him.

He chuckles. 'Yeah, of course I am. You know it. He's just a child. Let's do our best for him.'

We both sigh at the same time.

'On the bright side, Milo has Lloyd rather on the run. Not a bad thing. Lloyd could do with some exercise,' I say with a smile.

V

Lloyd spends a long time outside, but that's all to the good. I'm not going to intervene while they're happy playing. Milo already seems to like Lloyd, who is gentle and friendly, and also the most uncompetitive sportsman you will meet. He's let Milo win every game, but will make it appear as if he's just been pipped at the post. Young Milo beams like he's won the World Cup every time he makes a catch.

In they come, eventually, and Kendi and I clap and cheer and 'woohoo' Milo.

He's chuffed to bits.

'That's probably given you a bit of an appetite,' I say. 'All that running around!' He looks blank. 'Would you like a drink and a snack?'

He ignores me.

I look at Lloyd who squints a little and mouths, 'Is he a FASD boy?'

His face does not have the characteristic sloping features that a quick Google of the condition will identify, but he does keep his fists clenched. There are other explanations. It could simply be fear of a new environment, for example. But it's interesting that Lloyd's thoughts have already gone in the same direction as mine.

I shrug. It's too early to jump to conclusions. I will have to do a few more observations. I get the biscuit tin and open the lid. Like the pooches when they hear the rip of a ham packet, he looks up straight away, on high alert.

I literally see his nose twitch, as if he is sniffing out the smell of chocolate and sugar.

I lower the tin to his height and watch him smile and shyly creep up to it. I shake the tin so the biscuits make a rattle. I know the form said he was seven, but he's more like a four-year-old. He puts his little hand in and wraps it around four biscuits. We all look at each other and laugh. Milo joins in.

I offer the tin to Kendi, who pats his tummy. 'No, no, thank you. I will ruin my dinner.'

Lloyd points out that it's roughly lunch time.

'Oh, okay, well, maybe one.' He holds a chocolate Bourbon up to Milo and smiles.

'Would you like a sandwich?' I ask Milo.

He nods and says, 'Cheeeeeeese,' elongating the vowels.

'Please rhymes with cheese,' Lloyd says as though he's only just noticed.

'Cheeeeeeeese pleeeeeeeese,' Milo obliges.

I get the cheddar out of the fridge and realise that all

eyes are upon me. Lloyd, Kendi, Milo, even the dogs, and Mabel, Lily's cat, who has just parked herself on the corner of the table in a convenient position to join in the staring. I'm only grating cheese to make a sandwich, for goodness' sake. Anyone would think I was moving the King's jewellery. I feel a little self-conscious.

Sandwich complete, crusts sliced off and cut into triangles, I place a packet of Skips on the side of the plate. Milo sits down very quickly and bites into his food, tearing into the bread and smashing it into his mouth as though he can't get it in quick enough. He was clearly hungry. There are crumbs everywhere, but we can work on table manners later.

I can't help myself, and I know I shouldn't, but I do. 'Milo, did you have any breakfast this morning?'

'No, starving,' he says.

I turn around and make another pile of sandwiches which are consumed with equal energy and speed. He sticks the Skips one by one on the end of his tongue and laughs. He's a happy little soul, at least. As soon as he's finished, he pulls at Lloyd's arm to go out and play again. Lloyd obliges, even though he is looking a bit tired and has work to do. Off they go, escorted by Doug and Dotty, who never play with balls but love being near children. It's deliberate, the not playing with balls. They don't do it because I never taught them. I've had dogs before that play fetch. It's exhausting for the owner. One of life's tiny little wisdoms you learn along the way.

Kendi looks at his watch. 'Time for me to make a move, Louise.' He waves goodbye to Lloyd and leans out the backdoor to wave to Milo. 'Goodbye and lovely to meet you, Milo.'

Milo stops and makes an unreadable face. He looks at Lloyd. 'I staying here?'

Lloyd says, 'Yes, if that's okay with you.'

He makes another face and says, 'Yeah'.

I feel my heart sink. The poor little fella didn't understand what was happening today. Imagine not knowing when you are brought somewhere that that is about to be your new home. Was that Daisy? Sometimes new social workers or, in Daisy's case, student social workers, are too scared to tell the truth. Or if they do, then they time it for the last minute, then go, leaving the foster carers to pick up the mess.

Lloyd is trying to convince Milo that he could spend some time with me. 'Louise is good at playing catch, too. Shall we let her have a go?'

I've actually never seen a child attach themselves to Lloyd before with quite such ferocity. He's sticking to him like velcro. Poor Lloyd. I can read his face. It's saying, 'I've got tonnes to do, help!' as is Kendi's.

'Sorry, Louise,' Kendi says, 'But I must…'

I, on the other hand, never have anything to do, clearly!

I manage to encourage a rather confused, unsure little Milo away from Lloyd with the aid of Doug and Dotty, who absolutely adore the roles of foster carer assistants and are very experienced in this area. They round him up like a sheep and nudge him into the sitting room. I'm sure he needs to go and unwind with some toys for a little while, and maybe a spot of TV. But he just looks a bit bewildered. He is adorable, despite not knowing where he is or what on earth is happening to him. I do my best to reassure him while he strokes the dogs.

He beams at them and looks up at me, as if he is the discoverer of man's best friend. 'Dogs,' he says, pointing as though I might not know what they are.

The feeling that Milo is emotionally and developmentally much younger solidifies. He's spoken to express his needs over food, but his vocabulary is limited. So far he has spoken in words and partial phrases. I wonder if any adults have spent time talking to him properly. I hear Kendi and Lloyd saying goodbye out in the hall.

I say to Milo, 'I'll be back in a minute.' He isn't listening – too busy with the pooches.

I grab Kendi before he goes out the door. 'Can you get hold of any more information about where he has been? We need to know if he already has an EHCP.' The Health and Education Plan that will entitle him to certain things in school: additional support that I'm already certain he will need.

'And what about school?' I say, suddenly panicking that it's one of the things we haven't yet discussed.

He shrugs and frowns, 'Didn't Daisy say?'

I shake my head and remind him how quickly she departed after she'd fulfilled her mission and parked Milo here.

He goes to his phone and scrolls through his emails. He mumbles as he reads out, 'No school.'

I sigh. 'Right. Where did the last foster carers live?'

He carries on scrolling and says, 'Derby'.

'What?' My eyes are probably popping out of my face. 'That's miles away!' I think about Daisy again and I'm sympathetic once more. She had to fetch him from Derby and drive for a good four hours to get to us. She is clearly a new driver and she must have been very stressed. How damned irresponsible of the social work manager to do that to a young student. Good grief! But Milo's been stuck in a car for four hours, too. No wonder he wanted to be outside.

I ask, 'So *why* was Milo in Derby?'

Kendi stares at his screen and speaks slowly. 'Because he was with an agency and moved out of county, as far as I can see.'

'Why?' I persist. 'Why was he moved out of county? What's the story?'

Kendi sighs again. 'It's probably because of the shortage of foster carers nationwide. Kids are being moved all over the place.'

'So what about before that? Do we know if he was in any other placements before the last lot in Derby?'

Kendi says he isn't sure but will do some digging. 'Meanwhile, we'll need to get him enrolled into school here.'

We say goodbye and he rushes to the next foster family and their situation. He's like a supervising Superman.

VI

I return to the sitting room and find Milo playing with the toys from the toy box. Interestingly, he has chosen toys that toddlers play with. All the sensory toys. Crackle paper, fidget balls, the squishy plastic pig that I hate because it attracts the dog hairs and I have to wash it so often. Watching him tells me a lot. Everything I've seen so far fits along the FASD lines. I watch his hands closely and notice how he grips the toys.

'Why don't we take off your shoes and put them away? You'll be more comfortable,' I suggest.

He sits on the floor and wrestles with the laces. I hadn't noticed until now, but they seem to be double or even treble-knotted. Probably not the best thing for a child with his motor skills, or lack of. He needs some slip-on shoes to make him feel independent, I think, as I help him to take them off. I carry them out to put them in the hall and I'm surprised at how small they are. I check the size. He takes nine. That's very small. I'm sure Jackson and Vincent were in sizes one or two at this age. Maybe he has small parents. I hope Kendi gets to find out more for me so I can fit the parts of this jigsaw together.

'Would you like to watch some TV?' I ask, returning to the sitting room. 'Shall we see what children's programmes we can find you?'

He is enthusiastic about this suggestion, nodding yes. As if to prove the point, he sits down cross-legged and stares at the black screen. Then he puts his thumb in his mouth, waiting. I scroll through the menu and find a few shows. He points and waves at the thumbnail of *Bluey*. On it goes, and I can tell by his drooping eyes that he is tired. I'm not surprised after such a long journey and all the running around in the fresh air with Lloyd when he got here. I make a little cushioned area on the floor in case he wants a snooze.

'Are you hungry?' I ask, even though it's less than an hour since he chomped his way through the crisps and sandwiches.

He nods again. He moves his thumb enough to say 'Cheeeese sand wig.'

While I'm in the kitchen, I root through the cupboard looking for a cup with a lid. I come across an old Sippy cup. It's seen better days, but it gives me an idea for a shopping trip tomorrow. I fill it with water and take it in with the sandwiches, more crisps and some sliced-up banana in a bowl. He takes his thumb out and eats it all as if it was the first time.

I leave him to it. He is more than content, especially with all the attention from Dotty and Douglas. At some stage he will have to learn that the dogs are sitting staring at him because he has food, not because they think he's wonderful, though I'm sure that they are also enamoured of anyone new who will fuss over them.

I head back to the kitchen to clear up and ponder a little more about this rather peculiar young boy who has just entered our lives. If I didn't know better, I'd say they made a mistake on the forms with his age. I need to know more. Natural curiosity, yes, but the more I know, the more I can help him to better navigate what will undoubtedly be a strange, new world for him.

When I've finished I go into the sitting room to check on him and, as predicted, he is crashed out on the cushions. Arms akimbo on his back, mouth open, fast asleep. The dogs have clearly finished every remaining crumb as the little plate beside him is spotless. Naughty doggies, but they lie next to him like Egyptian greyhounds protecting the pharaoh.

By the time the children pile in from school, Milo is awake again, still sitting between the dogs, watching TV and holding the stretchy pig. As soon as I hear the door, I zoom to the hallway to catch them as they arrive. The process involves accosting them one at a time because, even though they all go to and leave the same place five days a week, they do not want to walk together. Lily has taken to meeting a friend on the corner and I think Jackson may have his eye on a girl, so will not be seen with his siblings. Vincent puts his earphones in and will listen to Jamiroquai all the way home, oblivious to everything else around him.

Lily and Jackson mock Vincent's love of funk and hip hop, but I love it. I am sure he tires of me saying, 'Oh, back in the day I always put Jamiroquai on before I went out with my friends.' I leave out the copious amounts of wine and mad dancing in my flat at the same time. He doesn't need to know that bit. Though he does find it funny that every time he puts his music on through the kitchen speaker I snap into funk dance mode. Or at least what counted for it the first time the band were popular in the early nineties. I shall ignore the fact that was 30 years ago and assume I've made some sort of miscalculation.

First in through the door is Vincent. He pulls the headphones out from his ears. 'Hello, Mum.'

I quickly explain that Milo is here a little earlier than planned.

'Oh, cool. How is he?'

Vincent is one of the politest people I have ever met. He seems to just 'get' the importance of small talk to ease the social passage of any situation, and does it very naturally. He understands why little things make a difference. He walks through the hallway, past the sitting room, then steps back to wave to Milo.

'Hi there, Milo, you okay buddy?'

I hear no reply. Perhaps he's engrossed in watching his

TV programme, or is super shy. Next in through the door is Jackson.

'Hi, Jackson. Good day?'

From my first-born, I receive a grunt. He seems to be a bit quiet or preoccupied lately. His head is down when he goes to and from school. I'm not sure what's going on with him, but he's an old head on young shoulders. Maybe he's growing out of education. Some children do. I explain that Milo is here and he makes a face that suggests that this information has somehow put him out. He walks to the sitting room and leans in.

'Hi, Milo, I'm Jackson.'

That's more like it. I was worried for a moment. I return to the front door to look for Lily. When I step outside, she is nowhere in sight. She has a key, so I text her with the news.

The boys soon release themselves from the restrictions of their uniforms. Neither of them like the school uniform, and like to relegate it to the floor or chair as soon as they walk through the door. I think they inherited my own view of school uniforms, which is, 'why?' I know some people think it looks smart and is good for the school's reputation, blah blah blah. Oh, and that it creates equity amongst the children, so that you can't see who is rich or poor.

Hello? What? Really?

Of course you can see who's rich and poor.

The uniforms some children wear, given the costs involved in purchasing new, are increasingly handed down or bought second-hand. The greyness of the white shirts, the sweat-stained collars and grubby cuffs, the scuffed shoes, the ripped backpacks. Beyond the uniform, the grown-out greasy hair and the smell of body odour continue the siren alerts. I think uniforms show up poverty even more than if teenagers were left to wear their own clothes.

Basically, when left to their own devices, it's jeans and hoodies. If they could wear non-logo and non-ripped jeans, they would quickly adjust to roughly the same clothes. I have seen older kids, county lines kids, outside the school, watching the students leave and walk along the lanes home. They are checking them out to see who to prey on. They tend not to go for foster children, because most foster carers put the child in their care in brand new clothes, get them to hairdressers and barbers and usually go mid-way on a brand. Most birth parents whose children have entered the care system will find the money to give their child in care an expensive hoodie or pair of trainers, even if they are broke. It's a way of showing them that they still love them.

No, it's the poorer kids, those living with single mums on benefits, that they go for. Or the wealthier, clean-skinned kids whose parents are naive and have raised kids who are easily impressed.

In a similar way, most foster carers are invited to attend training on child exploitation and are fairly clued-up as a result. But most birth parents, by contrast, are pretty clueless. Looking at Milo, I'm 100% certain that he isn't involved in anything like that, not even slightly. He couldn't be. He definitely wouldn't cut it as a drug runner – unless it was one that required taking a stretchy pink pig to complete the job. He has not let go of the pig at all.

I'm back in the kitchen when he appears in the doorway, dancing from side to side.

I say, 'Milo, do you want to go to the toilet?'

He doesn't respond, but I take him upstairs and show him the loo, lifting the seat for him. It goes everywhere, mainly because he will not put the pig down. I suggest we take his now weed-on socks off and rinse his feet.

He laughs.

I walk him to the middle bathroom which has a shower in the bath, excellent for sitting small people down and rinsing off their feet after a day at the beach, or soapy suds from hair after a shampoo. I notice that he generally walks on his tip toes and his toes are bent in. I've seen this before. It can be a sign of autism, and he does seem to have language delays, but with foster children we are never sure if it's neglect, autism or Foetal Alcohol Spectrum Disorder or something else. As ever, context is key. I recently read that, perhaps surprisingly, South Africa, Croatia, Ireland and Italy have the highest FASD prevalence. In the UK, it's estimated that around 4% of UK children could have symptoms consistent with FASD. That still sounds like a lot. By contrast, Bahrain, Kuwait, Oman, Qatar, Saudi Arabia and the United Arab Emirates – all countries where the production, sale or consumption of alcohol are restricted in some way – have no recorded cases of FASD.

I put the bathmat down and rinse off his feet. Milo finds it all very amusing, which is sweet. I dry off his toes and, like lightning, he flies out of the bathroom and downstairs back to the sitting room, where the boys are setting up Mario Kart. He slams on the brakes in the doorway, slightly wary of two much bigger, taller boys. But Jackson and Vincent are both little-boy friendly.

I hear Jackson say, 'Woah, there, little guy. Do you want to play with us?'

I watch from the hall, still holding the damp towel, intrigued as to what will happen next.

Milo tiptoes over to Jackson and beams at him, dancing from foot to foot. 'Yes, yes!' he says.

'Okay, little fella, why don't you sit there?' Jackson piles three cushions in a tower and indicates the spot.

Vincent, meanwhile, heads to the kitchen then darts straight back with the loot: several packets of crisps. The game is set. Jackson and Vincent sit either side of Milo, with the dogs flanking the big boys. I wish I had my camera!

They set Milo up with a controller and talk him through the basics of the game. He is super keen to get going. I head back to the kitchen and throw the towel onto the floor by the washing machine. I question myself then. Why did I bring it down to wash when I could have just hung it up? I know the answer. Somewhere in my psyche, some primal part of my

Milo's Story

brain is getting used to a new human and their body smells and all of that stuff. He is not mine, yet!

I pick up the kitchen mess that the boys have managed to make with such speed. There is no point in challenging them. They will use Milo as the excuse.

I check my phone to see if Lily has answered.

Her message is brief. Three letters: *Ffs*.

Oh, that's nice. Not.

I text her back and ask her where she is.

A one word answer: *Town*. I ask her what time she is coming home.

8.30pm.

I send back a laughing emoji with my message. *No later than 6pm. Dinner will be ready.*

She does not respond.

What is happening to our lovely Lily? Teenage hormones have a lot to answer for and I don't care what anyone says: in my experience, girls are much harder at this age than boys.

Take right now. The boys are happy to game, just be at home and eat. Meanwhile, Lily is out doing – I don't know what. She is at that stage where she wants to be *seen*. I get it, but it's terrifying. I certainly don't want her to be 'seen' by predatory men. My stepdaughters used to terrify me when we lived in Portsmouth. I remember Millie leaving the house when she was 14 years old with a push-up bra, the sort that have those chicken fillet things sewn in. I remember pulling the neck of her T-shirt up and telling her to be careful. I *know* that girls should be able to wear what they want, but the world hasn't caught up. It isn't like that.

Suddenly, in comes Milo, rubbing his tummy. 'Hungry.'

He really can't be, but I tell him that dinner will not be long.

He takes an apple out of the bowl and runs off.

In comes Vincent 10 seconds later. 'Mum, Milo threw the controller on the floor and now it's broken.'

I sigh and think to myself, and *here we go*.

VII

Within minutes, Milo is back in the kitchen complaining that he is hungry again. He must have eaten half a loaf of bread in the last couple of hours, but never mind.

I decide to go for a quick pasta dinner. There is still a French stick from yesterday that did not get eaten – not sure how, in this house, but even though it's going a little hard, it will serve my purpose now. I crush a load of garlic and mix it in with butter in a bowl. I cut into the top of the baguette multiple times, then load the half-cut slices with the garlic butter and wrap the lot in tin foil.

Then I put the oven on. Back to front, I know, but in my head that buys me more time to make pasta. I suspect Milo is pretty basic when it comes to food, so I keep his bowl of pasta plain and grate a lot of cheese to put on top. The boys like green pesto sauce and olives. I make theirs and call them in, remembering to plate up a portion for Lily to eat when she gets back.

'Dinner's ready!' I call again.

When I unwrap the garlic bread and start to pull it apart, it smells amazing. Not bad for the resuscitation of a stale reject.

The boys tuck in straight away, wolfing down their pasta. Milo sits on a cushion that Jackson has kindly thought to bring in, evidently recognising that Milo is a little short.

Milo eats all his pasta, but pushes his bowl into the middle of the table, knocking the salt and pepper out of the way. He climbs down off his chair and begins to run around the house.

I sense that the boys are bracing themselves for whatever is about to come next.

'Milo! Time for me to show you your new room,' I call out. He wasn't interested when I said it earlier, but now we need a distraction.

We meet upstairs as I catch him on the landing. Milo is excited to see his room. But only for about 10 seconds. He jumps straight on the bed and rolls around. Then he is straight back out of the door. I have a feeling that nap earlier may have been a mistake.

'Milo?' I call him back and, to my surprise, he comes.

'Would you like a bath?'

He shakes his head and scratches his bum.

'Do you need the toilet?' I can smell a sort of post-dinner cheesy fart. I take him to the bathroom. He sits on the loo with his trousers by his ankles. I pull the door to and wait outside.

'Are you okay?' I ask after a minute or two when he doesn't reappear.

I can hear some straining noises. I wonder if I need to increase his water intake. And add fruit juice to his diet. A few seconds later I hear lots of plops. I ask him again if he is okay.

He says yes, but I wonder if he needs his bottom wiped. I know he's way too old for that, theoretically, but I'm not sure, and I don't want him to get itchy. I decide that's probably too much for the first day, so I let him be. I have a pair of pyjamas waiting for him and, with a full Mary Poppins sing-song voice, I say, 'Time for your pyjamas.'

We walk up to his room and I detect a distinct waft of poo in the air. I literally do not know him well enough yet to ask about it in terms of washing and bum-wiping skills. I suggest he wears clean pants under his pyjamas. The best I can do for now.

Once he's in the spaceman pyjamas, he seems a little calmer.

'Do you want to watch a film before bed?'

He loves that idea. He grabs Stitch, his teddy, and walks downstairs with me. I line up a film for him. I direct him towards *Inside Out* because, goodness knows, this boy needs to do something about regulating emotions. And, if nothing else, it's nice and colourful even if it's a few years old now. I head back to the kitchen to tidy up. I check my phone and notice that it's 6.30pm. No sign of Lily as yet. There's no response to my previous message insisting on a 6pm return for dinner.

I message her again and use her preferred ploy of short and sweet: *Home time.*

I can see that she's read it, but she doesn't respond. Grrr.

Lloyd comes in and asks what we're having for dinner.

'Pasta.' I know I have some salmon and cream. I'm sure there is some asparagus left from Sunday dinner. 'Seafood vegetable delight.'

One of my gardener friends dropped off a bag of vegetables from his garden earlier. Absolutely wonderful. There is no doubt that home grown vegetables taste so much better than shop bought. Alas, I cannot achieve this goal. I have tried growing my own on a few occasions, but, if I'm honest, I get bored. I did manage an excellent crop of leeks one year, which at the time the boys and Lily loved. Cheesy leek sauce with home cooked ham or baked potatoes was on the menu for several weeks. Now they have moved on and prefer Italian food. And the growing of vegetables can be left to other people. And I'm very grateful.

I check my phone again. Still no reply from Lily. She seems to be focused on annoying me at the moment. I don't know why it's directed at me more than anyone else. I know that it's often said about girls and their mothers, but I am not her 'real' mother – as she recently reminded me. I'm still smarting, but don't want her to know how much that hurt me.

I get my sauce going and then go back to the sitting room to check on Milo. He is sitting on the sofa, smelling of poo, snuggled up with Dotty and Douglas. They probably love it: the cuddles and the smell. Tomorrow Milo will have a bath. I'll also take him to the big supermarket and stock up on Milo things. The film is underway and I realise with a sinking heart that this might be too near the mark for Milo. The central character, a girl called Riley, is moving to a new house and her sadness makes her joyful memory turn sad, too. Whoops.

'Do you want a different film?'

Milo shakes his head. I go and get his cup and fill it with water. I bring it back and sit on the sofa near him, not too close. I have to earn that privilege.

The bigger boys have already gone to their rooms to game with each other from the control rooms of their beds. I text them to do their homework. I text Lily to come home. This is how modern communication seems to work best.

After the film, I manage to entice Milo to clean his teeth, and the teeth of Stitch his teddy. You gotta do what you gotta do. Milo genuinely seems tired and quite relaxed, no longer so phased by his new surroundings.

But I'm alert. I'm not that daft, so, what's the crack here, Milo? It can't be this straightforward, can it? I sit on the chair by his bed and read him *Peace at Last* by Jill Murphy. It's another thing that's been around for a while now, but I simply could not get young children to bed without it and I always end up yawning and looking forward to 'Bedlington' myself.

He hasn't been read to, that's obvious. He doesn't understand the rules. Eventually he lies down in bed, and I make sure that the lights are dim. I use my best theatrical voices and he appears to nod off. So why on earth is he up five minutes later, putting the main light on and sitting cross-legged on the floor? It takes a good hour to persuade Milo to get back into bed and snuggle in. I read the book again, even slower than normal and turn the pages with exaggerated slowness. I make lots of sleepy noises along the way. It works!

I creep out of his room and pull the door to, leaving the hall light on so that the crack of light can be seen beneath the door. Finally. That was hard work. Phew!

I can hear Lily downstairs talking to Lloyd. Our relationship is changing. I'm acutely aware that I'm not always looking forward to seeing her, in case she bites my head off and says something else that's hurtful. Deep breaths. I Mary Poppins it into the kitchen with my brightest smile.

'Hello, Lily!'

She is 'busy' looking at her phone.

I point to the pasta and suggest that I can pop it into the microwave.

'I'm not hungry. I'm going to bed.'

Not a word about Milo from Lily. Not so long ago, she would have been the greatest foster-sibling hostess with the mostess. I sigh and look at Lloyd, who suddenly looks very 'owlish'.

Once she's gone, I say in a whisper, 'What's wrong with her? Is she okay?'

He makes a bit of a face. He still looks like an owl. 'It's very difficult for her at the moment. With the hormones and pressures at school we need to be here and be supportive. Probably best to leave her alone.'

Right.

I stand there, staring at him.

I see.

He'd evidently prepared that little goodie-two-shoes spiel. That's why he looked like a wise old owl – or tried to.

He touches my shoulder and says, 'I know it's hard for you both right now.'

I think I might punch him!

I see the bigger picture here. I see what's going on. He wants to watch the football undisturbed and avoid a row. Well, Lloyd Allen, I'll tell you now – I'm not going to leave her alone. I don't say that to him, because the last thing I want is an argument or to have raised voices, especially with little Milo asleep in his room, but it's the thought that's echoing loudly inside my head. I manage a 'hmmmmph,' and flounce from the room.

I take another deep breath and walk upstairs to Lily's room. I knock gently on the door and enter. She's sitting on her bed in the dark, with her coat and hoodie on. The hood is up. She's busy on the phone. The light reflects onto her face.

'Are you okay, Lily? Would you like something for dinner, or a sandwich?'

I hear a 'hmm' sound.

'Was that yes to the dinner or the sandwich?'

She looks at me, then quickly looks away. I can't tell you how painful this is. She was so much my little girl until just a short while ago. Now I feel that she hates me and I'm not sure why. It can't be coincidence that this has happened when that stupid social worker let her mum have full 24/7 access to her. Or can it? It certainly feels as if it has happened almost overnight. I'm uncomfortable with the whole situation. Even in this moment, I'm not sure if she's texting her mum or a friend, but either way she doesn't want me here.

Just as I move to the door she says, 'Can I have a hot chocolate?'

I turn my head back to her. 'Yes, darling.'

As I walk back along the hall, I notice that Milo's main light is back on. I walk up to the door very quietly and put my head around it to see what's going on. I'm confronted by an absolutely wide-wake Milo, sitting on the side of his bed holding Stitch, chatting about this and that.

'Milo, sweetheart, it's time for bed.'

He looks at me and I can see that his eyes are tired. There are great, dark bags under them and he has a sort of glazed look, but his body is still active.

'I'm hungry.'

Okay, so it seems that Louise's hotel and room service is busy tonight. He absolutely cannot, cannot be hungry after everything he has consumed today, but I shall play the game.

'What do you want?'

'A cheese sandwich and crisps.'

Hmmm. I've rather lost count of the rounds of cheese sandwiches he's had so far, but it's late now and a few hours since the last morsel of food passed his lips. He might sleep on a full tummy. He must be having a growth spurt.

Jackson and Vincent have both had periods where it has seemed as if they have hollow legs to fill, as well as stomachs. I head downstairs to be met by the sound of football. The volume on the television is up high, and augmented by the 'oooo, naaaaa, aaaaaw' commentary of the armchair football supporter. It stops for a moment and I hear, 'Louise, darling, can you get my wine?'

It's one of those little moments where I think, *what happened to my life?*

'Yes, darling,' I call, seething inside, my tone just sweet enough that the word 'darling' is loaded to communicate precisely the opposite to a term of affection. The subtlety, however, is lost on Lloyd, engrossed as he is in the game.

I supply them all with their individual requests, muttering to myself as I butter bread, warm milk and locate Lloyd's wine glass.

I sit on the chair in Milo's room reading to him once

more. Sure enough, the sandwiches are still going down at a rate of knots. This child is perpetually hungry!

After another story, I keep talking. I reassure him that the house is safe and the other children are lovely. They are really happy that he has come to stay, and so am I. I feel like a fibber when I think of Lily, but never mind. Needs must. I keep talking some more. I start telling him about my work and watch his eyes get heavier and heavier. All I ever need to do is talk about my work to send someone to sleep. That or B Roads. Perhaps I'll save that for tomorrow night. I tiptoe out once more.

I check in on the big boys, who both promise, on pain of death, that they have done their homework. I doubt it. Or, if they have, it was rushed so that they could get back to gaming each other. Whatever.

I go back to Lily's room, ready with the excuse that I'm collecting her mug. She is in bed, still on the phone. Even though Lily has been here for many years, I suddenly feel different about her and her presence. I know that I can go into the boys and say, 'Put your phone downstairs,' and they will. If I said it to Lily now, I'm not sure what would happen. Because Lily's mum bought her this particular phone we are now in a whole grey area that feels akin to walking on eggshells.

And no good can come of that. So I don't want to.

If I don't stand my ground and continue to behave like the adult mother-figure in this house, then who am I? Where will we be?

Time and time again, I've been in situations where the birth mother has undermined me as the foster mum. And I get it, let's be real here. Am I expecting birth mums to thank me and be grateful for looking after their children? When those children were taken away from them? I know the answer is 'no'. I don't know how many times I have sighed today, but I add another one to the count. I pick up the empty mug and say goodnight.

'And Lily? If you're tired and grumpy tomorrow, the phone will have to go downstairs.'

She says nothing.

I walk down to the kitchen. I can hear Lloyd's pundit commentary to himself. Before I reach the kitchen door I hear some movement in there. If that's Jackson or Vincent nicking crisps at this time of night… To my absolute horror, it's Milo. I look up at the kitchen clock. It's 10.30pm and this mama is *tired*.

'I'm hungry,' he tells me.

VIII

My eyes are stinging with tiredness. I feel dreadful. I stumble along the corridor to the bathroom, turn on the shower and look in the mirror. The face of an old woman stares back at me. Where did she come from? But wait. The old tricks are the best tricks. Before I go down that sad path of self-pity and self-loathing, I splash cold water on my face and smile.

Already looking 20 years younger!

In the shower and, after a positive chat to myself about how interesting and exciting life can be and how lucky I am, I get ready for the day. From our bedroom, I walk along the hall and peer into Milo's room. There I see a little sleeping angel. This is a vast improvement on what I was seeing last night.

A little devil is what I was dealing with yesterday.

After discovering him in the kitchen, he proceeded to run around the house, tipping the rubbish bins over and refusing to go to bed. He thought it was hilarious.

I did not.

Milo's Story

He was still eating at gone midnight.

Today I need to think about how to deal with this. It's not sustainable, not for another single night.

The boys are up and crashing about in their rooms. I knock on Lily's door. She is fast asleep and holding her phone, which means that she has been on it all night. I go towards her and say, as gently as I can, 'Lily, it's time to rise and shine.'

Her eyes open, like a little mole in the sunlight. She stretches and drops her phone onto the floor. I reach down to pick it up.

She screams at me, 'Don't touch it! Get off my phone!'

Woah, I don't know where that came from, or what makes Lily think it's okay to speak to me like that. I pass it to her and say, 'You need to get going or you'll be late.'

Lily is going away for five days next week on a school residential. The boys have already done this same trip and loved it. I suspect Lily will too. But for now, I just need to get her out of the door and off to school, where she can't be on the phone all day, thank goodness. I feel like I'm just kicking this particular football into the long grass. I'll retrieve it later.

The more pressing question is what I'm going to do with Milo today. Clearly, there is some detective work to be done. Something's going on with him that I need to get to the bottom of. And I absolutely need to get him registered at the GP surgery. I take a breath, as I know the reality of what that means. I will have to go in and stand in a line that snakes around the waiting area, almost squashing the poor people sitting down. It's the only way. I've tried access by phone a number of times and it has been ridiculously ineffective. Sometimes, when I press the ring back service, then wait again, and then do as the text message suggests and see where I am in the queue, I learn that I have not, in fact, 'call-back queued' at all. The brusque, 'if you require further assistance, please contact the practice' is decidedly unhelpful in those particular circumstances.

I think our GP surgery, which was taken over by an independent company, can itself be seen as one of the town's biggest causes of mental and physical health issues. I know people who have just given up trying to get through and get an appointment. But to what cost? Health is not something you can ignore.

So, I need to plan this carefully. I will have Milo with me, so standing in that queue might not be a good idea.

'Lloyd, do you think you might be able to watch Milo for half an hour later on this morning, while I go and stand in line at the surgery?' I ask.

Oh, we both know it won't be half an hour, but ever the optimist, me.

I have a yearning for a past where we phoned the doctor's, chatted to a cheery receptionist, got an appointment, sometimes with choice over the most convenient time of day, then went in at the allotted time and usually got seen within half an hour or so. Now it almost requires taking a day off work to navigate the system and achieve the precious prize of a face-to-face appointment. But there's no way around it. I have to get him in at the surgery – and the dentist, if I can find one within an hour's drive – and I also need the optician to get his eyes checked out.

This all used to be fairly straightforward and standard when a new foster child arrived with us, but, if I'm honest, any dealing with the NHS these days just stresses me out. God knows what it's doing to the poor people who actually work in it.

Worse than the NHS, though, the other organisation that is totally frustrating to deal with is CAMHS, the child and adolescent mental health service. Within the foster care fraternity we darkly joke that our children need a death certificate to get an appointment.

These days, when I have to work with both the NHS surgeries and CAMHS, I push my work aside and put the kettle on. It can take hours, sometimes days, to achieve anything. I hesitate to speculate about why it should be so difficult. I don't know if it's administrative incompetence combined with the way they seem to have decided to shunt most of the footwork onto the patient, but all it has done is create stress and contribute to loss of earnings. I wonder how much, across the national economy, this approach actually costs. Anyway, there's not much I can do but moan and vote. And neither thing is going to get Milo what he needs today.

Milo eventually wakes up and, guess what? He's hungry!

There is something rather sweet about him, but I can also see he has a 'side' to him, a side that I am trying to understand. While Milo munches on four pieces of toast with peanut butter and Nutella and a big bowl of cereal, I get on with tasks like loading the dishwasher and washing machine. I run upstairs to his room to gather anything that needs to go into the latter. He's thrown his dirty washing from yesterday onto the floor. I was so tired last night, I didn't notice it. As I pick up his pants, I stop and notice the skid marks. Not unexpected, but what is strange is the mark they have left in his pants. It's more sort of a blotch rather than a skid. Strange.

I turn on the machine, get myself a coffee and stare at the water and soap squirting across the circular glass window. It's my zoning out time: watching the washing machine. The same goes for putting the washing on the line. If it's windy, that's me gone. I'm mesmerised by the fabric moving about, blowing in and out. I'll happily stare at that for as long as I can get away with it.

Pretty soon after breakfast, Milo runs to the loo. I politely follow and wonder if now is an opportunity to begin the work of wiping the bottom and teaching Milo to do it better, so that he doesn't get the stains in his pants.

I hang around near the loo, wiping down the dust and a few dead flies from the windowsill nearby. I nip back around the corner and ask Milo if I can take some loo roll. I want to dampen it and wipe down the windowsill now that I've started. I lean past him and catch a glimpse of the inside of the loo. What I see makes me want to take a much deeper look.

'Shall I wipe your bum, young man?'

He says yes, so I gently wipe around the area, which looks sore. I have been here before with a child who had been seriously sexually abused. I wonder if I need to think along those lines with Milo. Instead, I change my mind when I look more closely at his poo. I see small thin off-white worms. It looks like he's been eating elastic bands. The poor boy literally has worms. This is not good, but it does at least explain why he smells of poo and eats all the time. If these things are left for too long, they can become quite serious. What was his last foster carer doing? Why didn't they pay attention? I decide that I *will* drive him to the surgery to get an appointment, because this boy needs to be seen by a professional.

Waiting in the queue is challenging, but I go armed with books and toys and ideas to keep Milo occupied. We stand there for the best part of an hour. Finally, when I reach the front of the queue, I'm told that there is a 2-3 week wait for non-emergency appointments, so they will email me a date and time.

Wouldn't people go to A&E for an emergency? I wonder. What constitutes an 'emergency' that *doesn't* require A&E? I'd love to know the criteria. Since I'm here, I put in a request to get an appointment with the paediatrician. I know from past experience that this is the best route to getting a referral to the educational psychologist. At least those wheels are set in motion.

In the absence of a doctor, I decide that my next best option is to walk to the chemist with Milo. On the evidence I have for what's eating him (literally!), we need to talk to someone today.

I ask to speak to the pharmacist, whom I've never seen before. They seem to have a different one every time I go into the chemist. She suggests a treatment for threadworm after I describe what I saw.

She also suggests that we *all* take it and clean the bathroom areas, and anywhere that Milo has touched, extra thoroughly.

'Because the eggs can live in the home for up to six weeks.'

How delightful. The others are not going to be impressed with this. It even makes me feel a bit creeped out, but at least we have confirmation and a solution. I'm so happy that we have resolved one problem, I feel victorious! #winningatlife.

Once home, I explain the scenario to Lloyd.

He doesn't look that comfortable with the whole 'worm' situation, but doesn't question taking the medicine. I put a kitchen roll and a bottle of anti-bac in almost every room. I'll explain to the others later. I wonder if humans can pass worms to pets? I take no chances and order a load of cat and dog worm treatments online. They will be here tomorrow.

Right. I feel I have done everything I can to deal with that particular aspect of things. Now we can carry on with the day.

I have begun making a list of things that Milo needs from the big supermarket. They used to have toys outside that small children could go on if you put a coin in the slot to make the outing a bit more interesting for them. No sign of anything like that now. Like so much else, they've been taken away. It's a shame. The boys used to love them. I wonder what particular aspect of modern life has put paid to that simple avenue of pleasure? Probably something to do with insurance and liability. I know I'm becoming grumpy again after my earlier buoyancy, but I do think that the world is becoming boring for children.

I break supermarket rules and pop Milo in the shopping trolley. To be honest, he will be far less trouble that way, but it's also clearly great fun for him.

'Wheeeeeee,' I say as we head off. 'Now, the only rule is that you are not allowed to stand up in the trolley. You have to sit down all the way round, and you need to keep fairly still in there, otherwise I can't push you.'

I hesitate before using the word 'rule' because Milo seems to have something of an aversion to them. To my amazement he does stay seated – even though it looks as if he isn't really listening to me. I've already noticed this 'not listening' – he was doing a lot of it last night. I'm a wife and a mother so I'm very used to it, but something about the way Milo doesn't listen is bugging me. It's not defiant, more like he's wearing invisible headphones. He only listens when I stand right in front of him. I wonder if he has a hearing problem of some sort. Nothing has been mentioned in the thin paperwork that's accompanied him, but then no one picked up on the worms either.

So far, I have plenty of questions and very few answers.

We pick up some trainers, some new brightly-coloured socks and a water bottle. I take him out of the trolley so that we can select new pyjamas and underwear and some more play clothes. He makes a beeline for the superhero-themed sweatshirts and T-shirts, so in they go.

I've noticed a direct link between children who are neuro-divergent and a desire to dress as a superhero. Not just dress up in some cases, but wear the costume all the time if they can. It's happened too many times to be a coincidence in my world. I wonder idly if anyone in the academic world has done a study on that.

Near the checkout, I pick up some packets of Pokemon cards. The boys will love teaching him to play with those. I go back and pick up some bath toys, including bath chalks that will safely wipe off the enamel. I hope that the novelty of them might lure Milo into the warm bubbly bathwater and that will freshen him up. I know it will help him to feel much better. A warm bath before bed is a good way for all of us to relax, and children who have ADHD really benefit from sensory calming. He's not quite ready for the whale music just yet, but I'm going to do everything I can to help this little boy feel safe and calm.

In the evening, it takes a good deal of cajoling, but I manage to persuade him into the bath. The bath chalks are a hit! He uses them to colour in the bath, I think I will have to come back to that with the bathroom cleaner spray and a new cloth later on. After a short while, there is hardly anything left of the chalks themselves. But he is having fun.

Having spent a long time getting him in, he now decides that he wants to stay there. I top up the water a couple of times when it starts to go cold, but eventually I have to insist that we are done.

He stands up and I wrap him up in his big green towel, then go to lift him out of the bath.

He slaps me in the face. Not a little playful slap, but a full-on whack. It takes me by surprise and makes my eyes water. I hold him by the shoulders and say, gently, 'Milo, that wasn't kind, was it?'

I learned a long time ago that it's pointless asking a child 'why?'

They don't know why they do things until they are older, and then sometimes their shame and guilt will be so big that they will have to tell themselves a new story, to enable them to live with it.

I wrap the towel firmly around him so he's not naked as he walks to his room.

'Can you put on your clean pyjamas?' I ask. I've already

laid them out on his bed so that they're waiting when he walks into the room.

He pulls them off the bed and throws them in the air, then runs around his room laughing. I wonder if he has snuck downstairs and eaten Nutella or something. He's a little wild and I don't know why. I think about what happened today. Not a lot if I'm honest, just the shops this morning and the supermarket, and a walk through the big park with the dogs in the afternoon. It has felt like a nice, calm, good day – so I'm confused.

'Can you put your pyjamas on?' I ask again.

'No!'

'Do you want to choose a different pair?'

He pulls open the drawer and tosses the clothes out onto the floor.

I feel a little cross but try to keep it calm. I'm the adult here and I know that I need to show Milo that I can regulate. Many adults lose their shit because they lose control. It's all too easy to slip into child mode, so I need to show him how to be grown up about things.

He walks directly up to me and hits me again. Insult is added to injury when he starts laughing once more and calls me names.

'No, Stinky!'

I'm sure that many patient foster carers would lose it now. I take another deep breath. I start to count inside my head, so that I don't reach boiling point. I feel my blood surging.

It's a strange mix of guilt, shame, anger and embarrassment. He is not backing down or changing his behaviour, so I do the best thing I can. I stand by the door and, with a big smile, say, 'Milo, when you're ready, you can come down and have a snack and watch TV.'

If I'm not in the room then he can't be horrible to me. The audience needs to leave and then the star of the show has no one to perform in front of. I go downstairs and leave him to it. As I go the laughter and name-calling stops. Very soon I hear nothing. A few minutes later he appears at the bottom of the stairs and says, 'TV.'

He's wearing the original pyjamas I put out for him, though he's got the top on back-to-front and the label is sticking out underneath his chin.

I call that a win.

IX

It takes a few days for the threadworm treatment to take effect. We are all fine, no signs of any of the rest of us catching them, but I have taken no chances. All the pets have been treated too, though it took several goes before I managed to fool Mabel into taking her pill.

Thankfully, the need to eat all the time appears to have subsided. My spray tells me that it kills 99.9% of all household germs. Do worms count as household germs? My level of disinfectant use must surely have got rid of any eggs. I feel the ick when I think of worm eggs in our home. But I convince myself that Milo is already looking a little plumper and a little fuller in the face. He could certainly do with it. He's so pale and thin, he looks like a Dickensian urchin.

I've noticed that Milo sometimes has trouble holding his knife and fork. In the cutlery drawer I still have the children's cutlery that the boys used when their little hands couldn't manage the adult size. Trying to use adult cutlery made them clumsy. Milo does make a huge mess when he eats. A significant amount of food ends up on him and his clothes as he tries to chase it, and items circle the plate and the table.

Milo can also be very impulsive and has few boundaries when it comes to keeping his hands and body under control. He struggles with his motor skills which might be an indicator of ADHD. If that is what he has then we'll have to wait a very long time for a diagnosis. That is only the first step. Even then it will require even more time to write the EHCP and submit it. Perhaps, if we get to that stage, it might be thrown out. That seems to be the norm now because, apparently, there isn't any money. Things have become so bad that this is also being said to the children themselves. 'No cake when you go to Costa with your social worker,' is what Lily was told. Then her social worker looked at me, like the children do, waiting for me to offer to pay. I ignored her. It seems a little wrong that they can spend 20K per week on an unregulated children's home per child, then begrudge a child in foster care a piece of cake.

In case you hadn't detected it already, I've become quite fed-up with children's social care – and CAMHS – and their presentation of helplessness. I don't buy the argument of no money. They are the 'corporate parent' and good parenting, corporate or otherwise, means that we protect our children and shelter them from adult stupidity. In the case of these two organisations, the stupidity lies with whomever is responsible in the local authorities for creating the dire situation of facing bankruptcy.

Most children in care have come from poverty, so having the corporate parent say 'there's no money' too is diabolical. It's not even true. There *is* money; we just have to find and direct it better. There is potential, and unlocking it, even if it looks 'different', is our role. We need to take agency; we are adults and, in many cases, in positions of responsibility and influence. We can and should use that to find answers – not repeat learned helplessness back at those who are genuinely helpless!

I come back to Milo, but all this nonsense affects him and will continue to affect him.

After another rather messy dinner, I decide I'll take him to the park to run off some energy before bed. My plan is simple. If he is naturally tired he will sleep better. His sleeping has improved, but sometimes when I go in to check on him, he is wide awake. Rather than getting out of bed and crashing about and waking everyone else up, including the dogs who start barking, we have agreed that a basket of toys can be kept by the bed, which he can play with until he becomes sleepy. Only a small selection, though; having too many toys achieves nothing. Children often don't play with all of their toys, they leave them sitting idle. I have learnt that just having a few out at a time seems to give them much more pleasure.

We head off down to the park with the pooches who have already been out today and think this is an added bonus, which it is.

We reach a nearby play area that used to be fenced off to keep the dogs out once upon a time, but our local authority, like so many, is broke. So, when the fencing needed repairing, instead of carrying out the repairs, they just took it away. Now children, dogs and poo are all together.

On the upside, it makes it a little easier when I have a child and dogs as I do this evening.

Milo loves the climbing frame and ropes; he's up there like a shot. There are a few other children with their parents and carers. Perhaps we all have the same idea at this childhood 'witching hour'. When Milo has finished the ropes, he heads off to the see-saw. He is crashing up and down on one end while the other end remains empty. The thought crosses my mind that I should sit on the other end, but there is a good chance that when I sit down he could be tossed into another town. To my joy, a little boy who looks about the same age as Milo (but is probably younger than him) asks to climb on as well.

'Is that all right?' a man, who looks like he must be the boy's grandad, asks. They seem quite content taking it in turns to go up and down. I stand by, chatting to the grandad who has plenty to say about how useless the council are and despairs that most of the facilities are in disrepair. He is not impressed at all. I make the appropriate sympathetic noises. Not difficult, because I agree with him.

Suddenly, Milo starts to go too fast and hard and scares the other boy.

'Milo, slow down! Milo! Slow down!' I request, in my firmest tone of voice.

He ignores me. In fact, my intervention only seems to spur him on. He goes faster and faster. The little boy is crying and wants to get off. I grab hold of the centre of the see-saw, look straight at Milo and shout 'STOP!'

The grandad rushes to help his grandson. I turn and say that I am so sorry. I hear myself say, 'Milo is my foster child,' and apologise again.

We head for home.

It takes an awful lot of energy to look after him. We do everything that we can to 'change the game' frequently. Lloyd takes a long lunch break so he can be outside with Milo for a bit, when the weather is good enough. Various outdoor toys and balls and games find their way onto the lawn each day.

'We're just running some energy off,' Lloyd calls to me, red-faced, as he comes into the garden room for the plastic racquets we use at the beach and I'm sipping my coffee in the kitchen glued to the laptop.

The next issue to tackle is the fact that he needs to be in school.

It takes a lot of support from Kendi, but soon everything is in place for Milo to start at a primary school in the local area. It's a drive rather than a walk away, but that's fine. He is generally okay in the car, as most children are. I say 'most' because a couple have grabbed the steering wheel or tried to put their hands over my eyes from the back seat. All therapeutic parenting goes right out of the window in those instances. I shout, pull over and then shout again. Life and death situations are, in my opinion, exempt from gentle 'there, there' language.

(I must say that neither of the children in question did it again after I told them off and explained, in no uncertain terms, how dangerous their behaviour was.) Milo, though, has so far been fine in the car. He likes to gaze out of the window and not speak. I can totally relate to this. I obviously need to concentrate while I'm driving, but I love staring out of train windows. It enables me to make a sort of private video with my own narrative running through. If I've got headphones on, it becomes a music video.

The school has offered Milo a staggered start, so he can go in just for the mornings for the first week, then go full time after that. I don't get the impression, so far, that Milo is an academic high-flyer, but nevertheless he still deserves – and is entitled to – a good education. I think maths and English are essential. If children do not pick up these skills and qualifications they will always hit barriers in life. It adversely affects their chances of prosperity, and that is not on at all. Milo has one more week at home and then the phased attendance will begin.

With Lily away on her school residential, there is at least a break from the confrontation with her, and I have more time to devote to Milo.

I realise that Daisy has not been back in touch yet. I wonder if she has even been back to the office. She looked so uncomfortable with the whole thing. It wouldn't surprise me in the slightest if she went back to her university and asked to transfer to another subject – marine biology or graphics – anything but social work. Perhaps I'm doing her an injustice. I hope so.

Milo hasn't had another bath. I can smell his pungent fumes around the house, as can the others. The dogs can too, judging by the way they follow him around, sniffing his derriere at every opportunity. I'm always nervous about new children and bath time. He clearly has an aversion to being clean, and I only hope it isn't for a sinister reason. Bathrooms and bedrooms seem to be the two most common rooms that abusers use. It's obvious why. I always leave the door a little open and I sit on the bathroom stool, chatting and folding things. Bath time and car time are the two spaces where the most disclosure happens. When you haven't got a notebook, you just have to remember and use the word 'gist' at the front of all reporting to allow scope for misinformation and mishearing of their accounts. He is such an unknown quantity. I have no idea what he has been through. As so often, the referral information was a joke.

I had very much hoped that finding and killing the worms would be the start of a new boy: Milo the incredibly well-behaved.

That hasn't happened.

In fact, as he feels better, his behaviour becomes even more challenging. Normally, behaviour is a powerful means of communication. If a child is unwell, their behaviour slips too. But with Milo, the healthier and stronger he becomes, the more testing his behaviour seems to be.

In the morning, while the boys are in the kitchen gathering their snacks, water bottles and packets of handy tissues, Milo comes in.

'Morning, Milo,' Vincent says.

'Hello, buddy,' Jackson choruses.

Milo responds with a sneer.

At first I think it must be a joking sneer, and he's playing, but very quickly I see that he is deadly serious. He marches up to them and squares up with a snarl, before punching each of them. I'm astounded when first Jackson, then his brother, receive a thump to the solar plexus – for no greater crime than saying good morning.

Where the hell did that come from?

Because of his diminutive size, Milo's punches at the boys are not hard and Vincent and Jackson make light of it. The whole thing is smoothed over, but this is a big red flag and a clanging alarm bell. The boys are tolerant, but it's not fair. This is their home, too. Milo's action just came out of nowhere. It was totally unprovoked.

I need to nudge Kendi to get hold of those bloody files. We need to know what we are dealing with here.

X

By 6am the next morning I'm dressed and at my desk. I haven't even let the dogs out of their night cages yet. I need to catch-up. I need to see what's going on in my working life. I've been spinning so many plates at once that, inevitably, I've been neglecting things, and because Milo arrived unexpectedly early, I hadn't even got myself into a suitable place to pause for a few days.

Consequently, I've let a few plates drop. Early morning seems to be a 'safe' time, given that Milo is so reluctant to settle down and actually go to sleep at night. The (exceedingly small) advantage is that he sleeps a little longer in the morning.

Before Milo came, I was busy trying to sort out a pilot programme for Spark Sisterhood, the charity I run for girls leaving care. We've worked hard to decide on the best course of action and have decided that I need to manage the behaviour of the girls. They are like a firework display, sparks in every direction.

I see two major barriers to girls getting employment and having good lives. The first one is the simple fact that most of them didn't do well in maths and English. Often, this isn't an indication of ability, but a reflection of the fact that many haven't even been to school for months, if not years. They are bright, but in ways that mainstream education does not understand. I am trying to find maths and English teachers who can work with me to teach these subjects in such a way that the girls do not know it's happening, and that employers recognise their level of maths and English as suitable for the workplace.

The other great barrier is sexualisation and sexual exploitation. The latter has happened to so many girls from all backgrounds. The ripple effects and nuances that flow from this could make a girl's life hell, and that hell will probably be in poverty, too. If this has happened to most girls in and from care, is this what people – or should I say men – think of them? As objects to be exploited? I can't bear this sometimes. It's a cycle of cruelty and exploitation. I need some time to think about it all properly, but with Milo, and now Lily, offering daily, and sometimes hourly, challenges, it's proving quite hard.

I know that Lily is struggling to navigate her complicated world right now, but it doesn't look or feel like struggling. It feels horrid. Before the residential she had started coming home later from school most days and refuses to respond to texts. She is vindictive and her language, particularly towards me, is incredibly harsh – ever since her mum came back into her life at 100 miles an hour via that bloody phone.

It's been nice to have a break from it.

I make a list of things I need to do in an attempt to stave off the feeling of being overwhelmed. Fostering can do that to you. My inbox appears to have gone berserk, but amongst the Spark Sisterhood related stuff, I see an email from Kendi.

He has forwarded an email from Milo's team at the local authority. I like his style of full honesty and transparency. He doesn't redact or mess with the messages. I have known some sharp practice over the years. If everyone worked with a genuine positivity and honesty we would all be thriving. It is an email from the manager telling him – not me, I'm only the foster carer, why should I be told anything – about Milo's social worker. It's sort of good news, I suppose, in that they are interviewing for a new social worker who will have Milo on their caseload.

God help them!

I wonder what that caseload will look like. At the moment, things are so bad that the managers are taking some of the cases. I understand why, but to me it's a terrible idea, because it exhausts the managers and takes time away from their management role. So it's good that one day in the near future Milo will have a trained social worker.

The other news is that I have to take Milo to have contact with his grandfather. It's in the contact centre, a shabby, depressing building near the fire station. The last time I was there I couldn't get the smell of damp walls out of my nose for days.

I email back asking for the details.

Contact has been arranged for the end of next week – a Saturday. I'm surprised. It's quite unusual, because not many children's social care buildings are open on a Saturday. I decide that (as I nearly always do, with younger foster children in particular) I shall try to leave telling Milo until the last reasonable minute. Little is gained by telling them too far in advance. It can send them into a spin for all sorts of reasons, as I'm sure you can imagine. And I'm anxious to avoid a setback when we've made some small steps of progress.

We've come a long way since the worming episode. There's no denying it was unpleasant, but I can't judge anyone for that, especially not Milo himself. Sadly, it's something that can happen with children who are bouncing around the system. Things get missed, or people are not tuned in to recognise these things and therefore they can be misdiagnosed. Everything in children's social care seems to be focused on behaviour first and foremost. Health comes second, even when the two things might actually be connected.

I email Kendi and the manager from Milo's team to tell them about the worms. Only now does it strike me that this has implications beyond the Allen household. I wonder if Daisy held his hand? We have no idea how long he had them for, and that means that the people he was living with previously may also have had – or still have – worms. The pharmacist was quite clear that it's something that needs treating and can become serious if not. I have a duty to let anyone know who's been in contact with him.

Milo's appetite is beginning to regulate, which is a good job because otherwise we'd have had to remortgage the house just to cover his food bill. He is definitely filling out more and has moved on to better food than the piles of sandwiches that were required in the first few days of his arrival. Already his hair is becoming thicker and he looks less sickly. I can't prove it, but I strongly suspect that his last foster carer, Michelle, fed him on supermarket meal-deals. I buy some for the boys and Lily to snack on when we take Milo out to the park and his eyes light up.

The other side of all this improvement in health, is that his energy levels are through the roof. He wasn't short of energy to begin with, but now he is becoming stronger by the day. And, my word, is his strength making itself felt. I have watched him lift my very large, heavy plant pots up. Normally moving them around in the garden is a two-person job.

He is becoming a regular mini-Hercules. Milo-Hercules will be his new name.

I confess, I am even a bit scared when he picks Dotty up. I panic because she looks terrified. Her chihuahua rounded eyes bulge like giant dobber marbles when she looks at me, pleading.

'Noooo,' I shout instinctively, and he drops her to the floor.

No one hurts my four-legged babies. No one. Poor girl. I sit her on my lap for ages after, reassuring her.

'You just have to be very careful around the cat and dogs,' I explain to him.

I don't blame her for being super wary of Milo as a result. There's always something to watch for when you have people in your home you think might be hurting your pooch. She just does a runner when he enters the room. It's another situation that I have to keep an eye on.

'Look. This is how you pet them,' I show him. 'And this is where you pick them up.'

I feel sick at the thought that one of them might lash out if they're being badly mishandled. If Dotty bit him because he was being cruel, I'd be forced to put her down. Doug is fine. He's still quite happy in Milo's company.

I am counting down the days until Milo can start school. Not for the first time, I realise how impossible it would be to homeschool a child, especially a primary-school child. I'd never get a break and would never be able to do any of my own work. I have met a number of mothers who homeschool their children and have become curious as to how that process is regulated. As far as I know, an Ofsted inspector will not go to a private home to do a review. If we're busy standardising everything in education, it seems odd that this is freer. We already know from the Covid pandemic what vastly different experiences children had of being homeschooled. It's all rather askew.

Vincent sidles in awkwardly.

'Um, So Jackson and me, we've been chatting, and we'd rather not eat with Milo anymore, unless we absolutely have to.'

'Is this because he punched you? I thought we'd got past that.'

'No. It's not that. We just don't want to eat with him because he makes disgusting noises and eats with his mouth open. You've seen him.'

I have, and I'm well aware that it needs addressing before he starts school.

'He dribbles and spits food over us,' Vincent continues. 'And all over the table. It's revolting.'

I sigh. 'We'll try a programme of separate meals for the next few days,' I concede.

Vincent nods. 'Good.'

He disappears from my door, duty as official delegate duly discharged.

Lloyd and I have stronger stomachs than the children, but Vincent's not wrong. It is pretty off-putting to eat at the same table as him.

When Lily gets back from her school trip, she soon starts her own anti-Milo campaign, bad-mouthing him at every opportunity. I don't want him to overhear her. She's just not very *nice* at the moment. I love her without question, but sometimes I'm not sure if I like her, or the person she's pretending to be right now. She's become increasingly snide and bitchy. Girls like her made my own brief time at school uncomfortable, to say the least. She's very grumpy, mainly because she's tired from her residential, but also from being on the phone too much, especially to her mum late into the night. I'm not sure what conversations she's having with her mum but it's uncomfortable knowing that we are probably being discussed.

I don't know Lily's family very well, having only met her mum briefly when we picked Lily up from contact a few times. They struck me as belonging on the set of *EastEnders* – they seem to love a drama for the sake of it, almost relishing it. Her mum has other children, half-siblings of Lily, who were also put in care, so the whole family has been split up. Lily tells me that now her mum has a 'new fella' in her life. My guess is that she might be trying to impress this man with her new-found insistence on 24-hour-parenting-by-phone. It must be a bit of a red flag when a man meets a woman whose children are all in care. My gut feeling is that Lily's mum is trying to present herself as a good mum. I just have a bad feeling about it.

The sad reality is that, as a foster carer, we can feel all sorts of strong emotions that get us nowhere. I think I need to begin to protect myself. It's another sad reality that it's usually the female foster carer who becomes the birth mum's target. I have never heard of a birth dad carrying out this level of manipulation and strategy. It's all very complicated.

I desperately want to be the better person in this situation, but, after all these years of feeling that Lily was my daughter and loving her so dearly, it's an emotional blow. I'm struggling. And it means that Milo and Lily are competing for my emotional energy.

The strain is beginning to tell.

XI

On Saturday morning, I wake Milo up with the news that we are going to see his grandad.

'Gandad?' He misses out the 'r' sound which sounds cute. 'Today? Now?'

I nod.

He springs from the bed like a leaping toad.

I laugh because his reaction fills me with delight. Not only in terms of comic value, but his sheer joy at hearing that he is going to see his grandad. It's wonderful to see. I'm also more enthusiastic than I was about this arrangement, despite it being a weekend, because I realise it means not unsettling Milo after his first week at school. He will have tomorrow to settle back down into the routine of the house and I will run his legs off in the fields before the Monday morning start.

'Yep. Straight after breakfast.'

'Wheeeeeee!'

This is great! It's lovely that Milo has someone in his life he is attached to and loves.

I need to remember that when I think of Lily and her mum, even when I feel Lily changing as a result of that intervention.

Milo whizzes downstairs to his little seat at the kitchen table. He is electric with positivity this morning. I'm now very curious to meet the grandad who can ignite this response in Milo and instil the best behaviour we've seen so far. He must be special.

He helps himself to a big bowl of Frosties, or actually, their supermarket brand replacement, because have you seen the price of branded cereals these days? I supplement this with several rounds of toast with Nutella and peanut butter. He wriggles off his chair and runs upstairs to get dressed. Before I've finished loading the dishwasher (it seems to be my turn again because, as ever, Lloyd does not seem to realise that to put the dishes *in* the dishwasher would probably take even less effort than carefully stacking them on the side), Milo stands before me as half-boy half-Spiderman, in some of his new gear from the supermarket.

I smile at him and say, 'Great choice. You look fantastic.'

Lloyd pops into the kitchen. 'Milo, how do you fancy learning to swim?'

Milo lights up, clapping his hands and nodding. 'Linemo.'

It takes me a moment to work out what he means. 'Like Nemo?!'

He nods once more. We watched *Finding Nemo* together a

few days ago. Very sweet. Although yet another story about a child who loses their parents.

'Great. I've booked you in for swimming twice a week!'

More clapping and nodding.

We haven't discussed this. I look at Lloyd with a quizzical eyebrow, as if to say, 'and who will be doing this?'

'Don't worry, I've got it covered. It's Tuesday and Thursday after school and I'll take him.'

I think out loud. 'Is that before or after tea?' His appetite has calmed down, but this young man still needs feeding at regular intervals.

'It's after dinner.'

I smile. 'Make sure you don't sink!'

This is all very exciting and it's lovely to see Milo so happy. Dotty chooses that moment to walk past, and does so without running from Milo. Maybe she has forgiven him – or at least senses that in a good mood he is no threat. We'll see.

I gather my bag and items for the journey, and we're all ready for departure. Or nearly. I dig out the booster seat from the boot of the car, though I have to scrabble around beneath the pile of clothes that I have forgotten to actually take to the charity shop. I've been driving them around for a while now.

Milo in. Music selected. And off we go. I have found younger boys to really enjoy the *Yellow Submarine* album by the Beatles. I think it's the appeal of the soaring brass instruments. You don't really hear them so much these days, brass bands and marching bands. It must be fascinating for children to listen to.

We pull into the Family Centre. I still always cringe when I read that combination of words on the sign. It is only a 'centre' for families who are apart these days.

I unload Milo, who is fizzy with excitement. I turn around and see an older man dressed in a pork pie hat, dripping in a ton of gold jewellery. The best-fit description I have for him is what we would once have called a 'Rude Boy'. He has tattoos everywhere and too-short, rolled-up trousers draw attention to his Dr Marten boots. To complete the picture, the trousers are even held up by red braces. Wow, he is a blast from the past.

The lyrics to *Mirror in the Bathroom* by The Beat pop into my head, unbidden. I'm transported in time. But this man has something edgier in his look. In my mind that way of dressing could sometimes go hand in hand with racism and violence. He looks, frankly, terrifying.

Until he smiles, and his mouth stretches into a broad grin. The warmth of his smile is utterly infectious and makes me rethink all of the judging a book by its cover that I've just shamelessly done.

He walks up to me, but Milo is already clinging to him like a koala by the time he shakes my hand.

'It's lovely to meet you, Louise. I'm Colin. Thank you for looking after this lad.'

He ruffles Milo's hair.

Grandad, or Colin, then lifts Milo up into his arms so that he can look him directly in the face. 'You're looking good, Milo.'

Milo is delighted with this assessment. It's all wonderful to see.

As we make our way towards the family centre, Colin carries Milo under his arm like a surfboard, while Milo giggles.

I see a familiar face hovering by the reception area inside. It's Pauline. She's been doing contact work forever and I should have guessed she would be the only one available at the weekend; she is a widow and has no family waiting at home.

Colin has evidently already been in before we got here, because there is a load of beautifully-wrapped presents all laid out on the table.

He holds his hand up and beams. 'Sorry, Louise. I hope you don't mind, I missed Milo's birthday when he was at Michelle's.'

That's the second time I've heard his previous foster carer named in the singular in conversation, rather than as 'Michelle and Andy' as they are on the referral form. Perhaps Andy worked away. I put that thought to one side, because Colin has also brought in a load of food. There are sandwiches, crisps, sausage rolls and cheesy biscuits, all spread out on little paper plates. He nods at Milo with another one of those winning smiles.

'Go on, son, get stuck in.'

Milo is beyond happy.

I stand back and watch the show — and what a lovely show it is. I am getting nothing but good vibes from Colin. He is a totally likeable character with an 'honest rogue' accent. He sounds like he's from Essex or South London, with a spattering of Cockney barrow boy thrown in...

'Do you want a cup of tea?' Pauline asks me.

'I'm not sure I'm staying. Perhaps Colin wants to have on-his-own-time with Milo?'

Colin smiles and says, 'Louise, look at him. I haven't seen him look so good in a long while. Anyway, I've brought biscuits, so stay, please?'

What an unusual and fun tea party we have.

We all sit on the floor and watch Milo eat his food and open all his wonderful gifts. He is loving life!

Colin, though he looks like a rogue, is evidently not. He explains that he is a retired fireman, now doing delivery work. He adores Milo. I want to ask so many questions (once most of the biscuits have been eaten), but I can't. It wouldn't be fair on Milo. This is his day, his time, and he doesn't need people around him talking about him.

As time passes, Colin hands me a little envelope. 'Only take this if you're comfortable, but I wanted you to be able to message me if you need anything.' He pauses. 'And I would love to speak to the boy occasionally?' His voice is hopeful.

I wait for Pauline to indicate to me whether she is

comfortable with this. I refer to the higher authority of a contact worker partly because I like her, but also because Milo still doesn't have a social worker.

'Thank you,' I say and take the envelope.

Pauline smiles. She does this work for the children, not the social workers. The contact time is coming to an end, so we all say goodbye. I look at Colin and know that I'm pleased that this man is in Milo's life. But where is Colin's son – Milo's dad? I *need* to know what his son is doing and why Milo's dad doesn't have a relationship with *his* son. I have to understand more about this situation.

I have so many questions.

XII

Back at home I tell Lloyd all about Colin. Perhaps I'm over the top in my description, because Lloyd is a little wary. I think he often balances my natural enthusiasm when I meet a nice person with a healthy dose of scepticism.

He comes in with, 'You don't know that,' when I make assumptions based on how Colin seems. I know, after a childhood of abuse, I already had a heightened antenna for detecting a good character. That radar has only quickened and deepened over time.

'I like Colin.'

I'm not normally wrong, whereas Lloyd has been misled on the odd occasion.

'You were blind-sided by the biscuits.'

'I'm a fan of people who dare to be themselves. Colin's ease with himself made me smile.'

Besides which, we're all flawed to some degree. When I know a person has particular faults and I have to work with them, I'll give myself the heads-up, so I know *how* to navigate the weak spots. It's the same with children, too. We make a great mistake if we think that all children are easy and uncomplicated people. They're not.

'I'm looking forward to meeting him again. And to finding out more about Milo's background. I'm sure he will spill the beans. In fact, I sensed that he wanted to but was holding back…'

Lloyd gives it another, 'You don't know that.'

I've been defending Colin, but Lloyd's right. I don't really know anything about the man, and he certainly has an aggressive appearance that might be off-putting – was off-putting, in fact – when I first encountered him.

Perhaps it's caused by Lloyd's insistence, but I start to have a bad feeling. Maybe my radar's off after all. There's no denying that Colin does have a very distinctive look. Neither of us want to think that Colin might be part of some of the more extreme right-wing movements. An ex-neighbour of mine was into the right-wing thing in worrying ways. He loved Hitler and the Nazi party. He had swastikas on display in his bedroom. He wore a Hitler 'World Tour' T-shirt and actually made hissing sounds near me after he learnt that my birth father was Jewish.

Both Lloyd and I have memories of the skinheads and the far-right groups from the 1980s. They would appear at peaceful protests and cause havoc. I can remember walking through Oxford one evening with my boyfriend and being jumped on by skinheads who called us 'student scum'. I was

14. They used to scare me because I was never quite sure what it was that they hated, especially when I was being targeted. Sometimes it felt like they hated everything. I am not good around people like this. It makes me feel unsafe and makes the world seem harder. I simply do not understand racism or homophobia, or any creed of intolerance. It's irrational and sometimes stems from some deep, pathological hurt. Or plain stupidity.

Colin's smile is disarming, but his presentation is unsettling and definitely brings to mind those dark days of the 80s. And, if he's such a good grandfather, why did his grandson end up in care? There's more to find out there.

Meanwhile, I must keep an eye on our little superhero, who is still high on sugar and life. Milo has set up his new toys from Colin on the floor in the sitting room. He is so proud of them. He has something called the Upside Down Challenge which involves putting on goggles which invert everything, so that you see it all upside down. He is thrilled by it for about 30 seconds, then he starts to panic. I take the goggles off him and give him a cuddle.

He's a little bit shaken. Seeing the room upside down has really unsettled him. I sit him on my lap and hold him tight. He puts his hand on my face and feels my cheek. He smiles and says, 'Grandad has a hairy face.'

Even with my middle-aged woman hormones raging, my face is not as hairy as Colin's. I pick up his goggles and try them on. I can see how this could be disorientating. I decide that I'll put them in the cupboard for now. I lift up another gift. It's a large box of yellow plastic toys. A modular toy set, which has magnetic connections. Lloyd walks in. Perfect timing.

'Oh, shall I help you start building?' he asks when he sees the box. 'Let's start with all the pieces that look like this,' he holds one up. Lloyd and Milo sit on the floor, laying it all out under Lloyd's instruction. Milo is engrossed and, as Lloyd sits down, Milo rests his hand on Lloyd's arm. That is so sweet.

I think Lloyd misses doing this stuff since the boys have moved on to hibernating in their rooms and only doing online gaming.

I look at the other gifts that Grandad Colin bought for Milo. They are all education-based toys. He's thought about it. He's trying to help, trying to do the right thing by his grandson. That doesn't strike me as very 'skinhead'. I can't equate the kind of person who would buy these sorts of toys with the ones who gave the 'student scum' a kicking in my youth. Colin's got to be a good egg. Hasn't he?

Lily is off out. Before I have a chance to say, 'Where are you going?' the door is closed. I make an attempt to leap after her, then feel like a lost puppy walking away from the door and into the sitting room to glimpse her walking up the road through the window. I notice that she is wearing new clothes. Not things that we bought her. And in a new style, too. She used to be into a bit of vintage boho and Lana Del

Rey lace, frills and pastels. Now she is in tight tracksuits and sports hoodies. I wonder where the new clothes are coming from. Her mother again?

'What are you doing staring out of the window?' Lloyd asks.

'Lily's wearing clothes that we didn't buy her.'

'I'll check her card to see if she bought them.'

We top up her card every Friday. It was her pocket money once. Now we call it an allowance. I feel sad once more, because I sense more of the invisible threads that used to hold us together break as she pulls further away. I know it's totally normal for teenagers to do this, but because I'm a foster mum I also know that I have no rights and no claim on her. It's heartbreaking.

To distract myself from thinking about it anymore, I leave the boys to it and pop upstairs to sort out the bathrooms and see what Jackson and Vincent are up to. I look in Lily's room. All her trainers and boots are neatly lined up as normal. Nothing is missing, so what is she wearing on her feet?

I look around her room at the clothes on the bed and floor. It's a mess. I begin to scoop them up and put them on hangers and back into her wardrobe. I pick up what looks like a clean blanket that has been flung on the floor and return it to the bottom of her wardrobe where I find a box. I open the box and discover three vapes.

I tell myself over and over that this is all normal teenage behaviour and try not to get upset about it. Rebellion is to be expected, and if this is the form it takes, then so be it. I was doing worse at her age. And of course she's going to start hiding things from me. From us.

I finish tidying up and realise that me doing this is a little way of showing her that I love her. I feel out of step, wrong somehow. I can't compare myself to a mother; the law and the system does not say that. At the same time, when we started fostering we were told to treat children as our own. We've always tried to do that. Still, when shifts happen like they are with Lily, the reminder that they are *not* our own is stark. If I try to intervene, I know that I will soon be reminded by the social workers and the birth family that she is *not* our child. The system wants it both ways, as ever, but no one can have it both ways.

Several hours later, Lily still isn't home. I try not to be cross and just compose a text to check in and make sure she's ok. I keep the tone light. I'm finding that I text her too often these days. It's easier than talking to her. I word my messages carefully, partly because I don't want to say anything that will upset her, but also because I'm not entirely sure that she's the only person reading them. I no longer feel entirely confident about what she's showing to her mother… It honestly wouldn't surprise me if she was sending them to her mum. I hope not, but as Lloyd would no doubt happily tell me, 'You can't know that.' But I know only too well how easy it is for words to be twisted and for judgements to be made.

Hi Lily, I hope you're having a nice time. What time are you home?

I read it back and get annoyed with myself. Should I really have to be gently asking a stroppy teenage girl what time she is coming home? Or should I instead tell her what time she *must* be home? Parenting teenage girls is so different to parenting teenage boys.

The second text has a more business-like tone, reflecting the fact that I'm fed up.

Hi Lily, please be home no later than 7pm.

After all, it is Saturday and she has been gone all day and I haven't a clue where she is. I may have to try the Apple tracker. We've resisted until now, but I'll look into it. I just want to know that she's safe.

There is no reply.

At around 8pm she returns, but goes straight upstairs and closes her door behind her, very definitely shutting us all out.

'Hi Lily, would you like some dinner?'

I wait for a while. Eventually she says, 'Naaaa.'

And that is the full extent of our Saturday interaction.

Sunday is a busy day. I leave everyone at home while I dash to the big supermarket to pick-up a few last bits for Milo, so he has everything he needs for school tomorrow. I leave early so I can get there when it opens. I find a Spiderman backpack and a mini lunch box, not that he will be there for lunch in week one, I remind myself, but we can fill it with fruit and snacks like carrots and cucumber to keep him going through the morning. I'm trying to get him into healthy food as much as possible.

Lloyd takes the older boys and Milo out for an adventure walk up to the big hill, which is a 20-minute drive away. They have so much fun and Lloyd sends me pictures of them all laughing and running around playing a game called 'Catching Leaves'. The rules are very simple. You just stand in front of a tree with the wind blowing at you and see if you can catch leaves. It's great in autumn. And much more difficult than it sounds. I'm so pleased they've had a nice time. They needed a day like this.

How was Lily this morning? I text. I didn't see her before I left.

She went out.

I ask where and who with.

Not sure but she went straight out after you left the house.

This is not normal behaviour. Lily likes a lazy morning in bed on a Sunday. Now she's up and out by 9.30am? Really?

Then it occurs to me that maybe she has a boyfriend. Maybe I'm barking up the wrong tree thinking that this is all to do with her mum. That might also explain the secrecy, the change in style, the extra make-up.

But then I immediately feel hurt that if she does have a boyfriend, she hasn't said anything to me. Perhaps she is telling her mum and asking her for advice and not me. Am I jealous? I think I am. Good grief, this is complicated, I don't want to be jealous. I want to be kind and open and friendly, but I have, in my head and heart, been Lily's mum for a long time. I have fed her, been there for her, nursed her when she was sick, bought her first bra and celebrated her period with lunch and a shopping trip. These are all the things a mum does.

I drive home in a state of gloom, until I have a stern word with myself just as I'm turning into our road. 'You are a foster carer. Your job is to do right by every child who enters your life, no matter how long they stay.'

Okay, I'm back!

XIII

After half an hour or so, I hear Lloyd's car pull up in the driveway at the rear of the house. In through the back door burst three young men and Lloyd. Milo is clearly very excited as he crashes into the kitchen wielding a big leaf that he caught, and a long stick. Vincent and Jackson always brought sticks home with them from walks in the countryside. What is it with boys and sticks? I have to encourage him to part with it when he starts to hit everything though.

'Milo, let's play Minecraft,' Vincent suggests.

They all shoot off. Lloyd is still chuckling to himself, presumably at something that happened on his walk. I point at his feet, indicating the muddy boots.

'The boys took theirs off before they came in,' I say, my reprimand clear by implication.

To be fair, the boys' boots are scattered in multiple directions across the conservatory, but still.

Lloyd makes a face, not unlike a child's retaliation.

'We had great fun and went to McDonald's on the

way back,' he begins explaining, while wrenching off the offending boots.

He only has the first one off before Milo storms out of the sitting room and flies past into the garden. I can hear angry boys' voices raised behind him. Milo is good in outdoor spaces but definitely struggles to be indoors. I need to remember to tell his school this when I drop him off in the morning.

Vincent comes into the kitchen. 'Why is Milo such a c***?'

I give him a serious look and he apologises.

'But he's been messing with my gaming stuff. That's another controller broken.'

Vincent takes gaming very seriously, way more seriously than Jackson. I never know if it is good that he has such strong reactions to it, or not. As soon as he is off the game he is delightful, back to being polite and lovely, but I wouldn't want to cross him in the middle of a game. Jackson has never been as uptight as Vincent. But the writing was always on the wall. When they were little, Vincent lined up all his cars and trains and got cross if anyone moved them. It's just the way he is. Isn't it great that we're all different? Which is another thing to tell myself with regards to Lily. I must stop taking everything to heart.

Milo runs around the garden for a bit, then goes back into the sitting room. He plays with his yellow toy set behind the boys on the floor. This is interesting. Milo evidently wants to be near the bigger boys but is not quite sure how to be. That's a hopeful sign. I don't know quite what to do with the information yet, but it's good to know.

Lloyd says that he's been thinking more about Colin. 'So, I took the liberty of having a quick look at his Facebook page.'

We both know that stalking is necessary to keep children safe; it really is… sometimes.

'I don't particularly want to have my suspicions confirmed, but I think there were white supremacist fists and far-right imagery.'

My heart sinks and I feel the muscles in my stomach clench. Exactly what I feared. Dreaded.

I open my laptop and search for Colin's name. I turn the laptop around and show Lloyd.

'Do you mean this Colin?'

Lloyd squints. He's not sure. I move the screen closer and ask him to put on his glasses.

He smiles and says, 'Aaah.'

Colin's friend list is a diverse bunch, I'm pleased to say. The fist Lloyd spotted was above a black fist and a quote by Rosa Parks: *You must never be fearful about what you are doing when it's right.*

Trust your instincts, Louise!

After dinner I do the usual Sunday evening rounds, checking that everyone has everything ready for the week ahead. I'm batted away. Everyone has everything they need, or so they tell me, but Lily doesn't take kindly to my gentle enquiry.

'Can you just do everyone a favour and get out of my face?'

Don't bite, Louise, don't bite.

I bite my lip instead.

I take Milo upstairs. 'Now, Milo, it's a big day tomorrow,' I explain, 'So you need to have a bath and get into your pyjamas. We'll lay out all your uniform and get your new school bag packed and ready tonight, too, so that you're all ready to get dressed and start school in the morning.'

It occurs to me, now that he doesn't appear to be a far-right lunatic, that I could message Colin and see if he wants to speak to Milo before school. He might want to wish him good luck. That would be a nice way to end the evening.

Once Milo is in bed, I bring my phone. A few minutes later it rings, as arranged. I pick it up and put it on speaker phone.

'Hello?'

Colin's voice fills the room. 'Hello, Louise, is Milo there?'

I watch Milo's face light up.

'Would you like to speak to Grandad?' I ask him.

He nods fast and hard and holds his arm out. I hand him the phone and he suddenly goes shy. I let them chat away while I lay out Milo's clothes for the morning. After a few minutes, Colin's magic works and Milo seems more confident and at ease.

'Now, son, I'll be thinking of you tomorrow when you go to that school. You make sure to be a good boy for all those teachers. You go and knock 'em dead!'

I tell Colin that we are reading a story now and that Milo will speak to him tomorrow, to tell him how he got on. We say our goodbyes. As soon as Milo starts the big wide yawns I close the book and tuck him in. I kiss him on the head and say, 'Sleep tight.'

I text Colin to thank him for doing that.

He messages straight back. *Thank you, Louise. I hope he has a good day tomorrow.*

So do I, I think to myself, so do I.

I'm awake at 5am, in spite of the darkness outside. Anyone would think I had a paper round. I get out of bed and decide to see this as an opportunity to get ahead for the day. I need to be out of here by 8am to get to the school with wriggle time for Milo to start his first morning. The first thing to do is email the headteacher with my observations so far and possible solutions, or at least what's worked for me, to help with some of Milo's more erratic and unusual behaviour(s). Of course, once I've opened the dreaded email inbox I find plenty of other things to respond to and keep me busy. I get through an hour of admin and definitely feel like I'm stealing a march.

Next I walk the dogs. This is a little early for them, too. I think they're still in shock. Dottie has some of her breakfast and then takes herself back off to bed.

When it gets to 7am, I go in to wake up Milo. In fact, he's already awake and sitting in his bed playing with some of his yellow toy set. I'm glad I hid the upside-down goggles. I pull back his curtains.

'Morning, Milo. It's time to get dressed, have your breakfast and get to school.'

He is excited and jumps to it.

There is the usual Monday morning kerfuffle of looking for socks and shirts, in spite of my checking the previous evening. 'Have you got everything you need ready for school tomorrow?' was met with a chorus of 'Yeahs', which have now been exposed as fibs. It doesn't seem to matter what I do, every Monday morning is still utter chaos.

Lloyd is already on a call to Switzerland and cannot possibly break away to find Vincent's PE shirt, which is no doubt in the pile of clothes that I brought up to him which have probably now slipped onto his floordrobe.

I can't worry about them all this morning, so I smile and take responsibility for Milo. Once I've checked that he has everything he needs, we leave the rest of the Allen household to it and drive off into the busy morning traffic to another town to get him to school.

I wonder how much the taxi will cost for this going forward. Mind you, let's not get ahead of ourselves, that would require a social worker to bid for it with management first. That stage of the process could take months and I shan't hold my breath. In the meantime, I'm not at my desk working and earning money. I'm on 80p an hour with a travel allowance of 30p per mile. But, I reflect, at least I have Kendi these days. His persistence is another one of his many qualities. I know he'll sort it out.

Previously, when we were with the local authority, I'd begun to feel a little bit of work-creep coming on. I know it was because they were broke and short-staffed, but it seemed as if bit by bit some of their work was being dumped onto us. One social worker texted me to ask me to make an appointment with the child's school for him and the teacher. Not too onerous, you might think, except that this was a meeting I wasn't even going to. That's when I began to think no, this is getting silly, and started to put my foot down. I have enough to do, and I absolutely see my role as *children* first. My focus is on them, not doing admin for social workers or anyone else.

We pull into a parking space in the visitors' section of the school car park. I can see Milo's face reflecting a mix of his excitement and fear. Poor boy. I hope he finds a friend today. I open the door for him and help him out with his backpack. I hold out my hand and he grips onto it very tightly. Before we go in, I crouch down and put both arms around him. 'You are a wonderful boy and we all love you. Your grandad loves you. You are going to have a great morning, and I will be back here at 12 to collect you in time for lunch.'

We buzz our way in and say hello to the lady behind the reception desk. She is very glamorous for a school receptionist, or perhaps that's my own stereotypes and perceptions coming into play.

When she steps out from behind the desk in a cream suit and high red heels, Milo seems mesmerised by her.

'Welcome, Milo,' she says, cheerfully. 'We are so happy that you're here.'

She shows us to the chairs in the entrance area and asks me if we would like a drink. I decline her offer, tempting though a coffee would be, as I can see a queue forming by her area.

Milo has now switched his focus to all the photographs that adorn the walls in the foyer. They're images of happy teachers and students and suggest all the fun days they have inside and outside the classroom. There are also large paintings in frames of the children's work. I'm impressed by that. It's a lovely touch.

Out steps the headteacher. She's a rather round lady in her forties with a wide, welcoming smile. She is dressed in a flowery dress that pulls too tightly across her chest. I sympathise internally, because that happens with me too. I buy shirts and dresses with buttons and they always gape just by the bra, like a little window into what colour we have on today. I'm sure they used to put a discreet popper between the buttons once upon a time.

'It's lovely to meet you, Milo. I'm Mrs Seymour.' Her voice is warm and kind. She takes his hand and leads him towards the double doors that mark the gateway to the main school. Surprisingly, he doesn't seem to notice that he has his hand in hers.

The doors fling open with a wave of her pass, and off they go. Milo is swallowed up into the abyss of the education world.

I don't know quite what I was expecting to happen, but somehow the first week of half days at school goes okay. Ish.

And by okay, I mean that Milo isn't actually sent home, and is allowed to return the following week, although I have my doubts about the good it will do him. I have a debrief every day with Mrs Seymour about the morning's progress. It seems that every day something upsets Milo and makes him react.

'He's easily triggered,' Mrs Seymour explains.

Oh, how I hate that term. He is not a gun, he is a little boy who is struggling to regulate and understand his world.

'How so?'

'He punches and kicks other children for very little reason.'

'Can you give me an example?'

When I actually begin to deconstruct her sentences and get to the bottom of what's actually happening, it's clear that there is a pattern in both time and circumstance. Working with children who cannot articulate their feelings precisely *because* they are children, requires a certain amount of detective work to understand what's going on for them. I hate the fact that the school is already trying to shove Milo into a box.

My opinion of the school, after all the early good signs on the first day, has already begun to drop. It's a sad reality that often schools that look after children in the care system see one or 10 minutes of dysregulation and in their heads that's the whole narrative for that child. The 10 minutes of disruption comes to represent the whole day. They are 'disruptive'. They are 'easily triggered'.

I've had no word back from the doctors' surgery about a paediatrician or educational psychologist as yet, so I chance my arm and ask Mrs Seymour to set up an appointment for him.

Do I imagine that she suppresses a laugh? 'I'm afraid that you will need to take that up with the local authority directly, through Milo's social worker.'

But Milo doesn't have a bloody social worker. It's a Catch-22 situation.

After five days of this, I definitely have that Friday feeling. As we head out of school, I take Milo to the big supermarket. Too late I realise that, of course, he hasn't had lunch yet, so we're doing it on an empty stomach. Never a good idea when doing a food shop. This will cost a fortune, no doubt.

I'm troubled about what the future holds for him. He currently holds no EHCP, the Educational Health Care Plan that is a magic passport to the entitlement to support with his learning. I'm not a medical professional, but I think Milo is neurodivergent and probably has a host of other issues going on. The schools who have already failed him should be held to account for hurting a child's life.

If you've ever met the parents of SEND children, you will know that they are exhausted. Not because of their child, but because of the constant battles within a system that seems to routinely say, *No, you are not having the money or access to the support that you are entitled to.* More and more children have SEND issues as our society pumps more poison and crap into its blood stream. Too much booze and drugs, recreational and prescription, too many chemicals in processed food, pollutants in the atmosphere, all mixed in with the toxins of a digital age.

How many children with ADHD end up in prison? Too many, and that's the real crime. I realise that I'm ramming the trolley around corners with fury as I work myself up thinking about all this. Milo is not my child and has only been with me a short time. What must it be like for families who have been fighting these battles for years? I try to calm myself down as I put packets of nibbles, hummus and goodness knows what else into the trolley. Three quarters of the way round I have to take Milo out of the trolley, because there isn't enough room for him and a weekend of comfort food.

My rage is futile. By lamenting the world itself that we have brought children into, I achieve nothing. Instead, I have to act – for Milo's sake.

A starting point will be to find out from Colin about what's going on. How exactly has Milo ended up in the care system? Something dreadful has happened in his family. I know it. Like the flooding that now affects my home each year, its roots are man-made.

I drive the trolley down the toy and homeware sections and buy far too much for everyone, including myself. I read the description of a room scent and pop it in the trolley because it says it 'produces happiness'. I'm not sure that retail therapy is the answer, but I need something right now! I go to the checkout and panic as the zeros appear on the till. Oh well, it's only money. I ignore the nagging little voice that tries to remind me that this little lot has cost more than the equivalent of a week's fostering fee.

I want to go home, cuddle my children, eat too much chocolate and drink some wine.

XIV

The season moves on. Somehow we are suddenly plunged smack bang into the grip of autumn. It feels like not five minutes ago we were having al fresco meals in the garden, and now we are battening down the hatches against wind and rain. Autumn means putting the flood gates up and filling the sandbags.

I didn't sleep well last night. Everything feels so complicated and like such hard work. The way Milo's symptoms manifest themselves in resisting bedtime, not responding to instructions, running around the house incessantly – it's all exhausting. So much of it is not his fault, but that doesn't stop it from being challenging. Coupled with the battles to try and get him what he needs, it is overwhelming. Tiredness puts me into a low mood. It's a vicious cycle, because I know that my low mood is to blame for it all feeling more of a challenge than usual.

I sit in my office, keen to at least make the most of my insomnia by stealing a march on some work and life admin.

I come across a letter from the NHS inviting me in for my cervical screening. On the front of the accompanying leaflet is a picture of a group of women who look remarkably like social workers. I received this leaflet back in the summer, and tried straight away to do the right thing, even though there is nothing very much to look forward to in booking a smear test. But every time I phone my surgery to book an appointment, I fail to get through. This morning I'm delighted to discover that I am 'number one' in the queue. Still, I wait and wait and I am number one for over an hour, and then I'm cut off. Yet again I must drive to the surgery to see if I can get an appointment. I put the leaflet back in the kitchen filing system. It will resurface and remind me at some point.

I have put Milo on the dentist's 'new patient online' list, as I was told to when I went in. I have read that there is a two-year waiting time. These are children, for goodness' sake. How did we ever get into this position? Why can't we get a dentist for a looked-after child? They should go straight to the top of the queue. I have seen inside Milo's mouth as part of my home-based medical check. I didn't see any abscesses, but his teeth certainly need attention. The advice I was given by the receptionist at the dentist was to tell children to 'spit but not rinse' after they clean their teeth, so that the fluoride works. Well, that's all right then. There you go. Soon we'll have advice on how to fit wooden pegs or dentures.

Before I disappear down the fatal 'what's the world coming to?' rabbit hole that is clearly threatening to engulf me, I take what I hope to be some positive action. I sit at my laptop and prepare emails about Milo's education – or lack of it.

I take some comfort in the knowledge that, in spite of Mrs Seymour's less-than-enthusiastic assessment, Milo looks forward to going to school. This is important. I need to keep him there, however challenging his behaviour appears to be. If Milo does not stay at school – and the way he's going that wouldn't surprise me – he will be here with me all day. After experiencing a few foster children recently who should have been at school, that absolutely won't work for me. There is no way I can afford to sacrifice my livelihood for another child or, in fact, to save the local authority from spending money on a child that it should be duty-bound to. It's like working with the devil.

I don't see all the problems that the school sees, apparently. Absolutely, he requires hard work. There's no doubt about that. I couldn't agree more. Which is precisely why he *needs* the EHCP to extract more funding and support. Chicken and egg.

I send another email to Mrs Seymour with words to that effect.

She replies that the school simply doesn't have the capacity to write a request for an EHCP. She suggests that I should try.

But I'm not a teacher and not a social worker. And oh, have I mentioned that he hasn't actually got a social worker?

I understand that schools are overwhelmed with children who are struggling. Parental neglect, abuse and now food poverty is dumped on the schools. I know teachers who personally fund food for those in their charge. They bring in clothes and toys for the children from home.

They have to. Social workers are thin on the ground as the job becomes increasingly challenging with fewer resources and worn-out staff and managers. Sometimes I think we are already living in a dystopia. The future's here and it's bleak, it's unsustainable, and poor Milo is caught up in it all.

Next, I send a firmly-worded email to Milo's manager encouraging them to pull their finger out. Do something. At the very least, engage. I cc Kendi in. Milo needs a social worker and now! Kendi is doing his best without damaging the working relationships he has with us and the local authority. What a mess it all is. This boy only has us, his grandad and Kendi making sure that he is okay.

I send a message to Colin to keep the lines of communication open. In spite of Lloyd's initial misgivings about him, I want to believe with all my heart that he is a good influence and someone that Milo can depend upon in the future. After all, who else has he got?

Lloyd is becoming frustrated with me because I spend so much of my time going around in circles. He's sick of hearing me moan about what he already knows. Kendi is kind and says all the right things but, after a while, his words slip into platitudes.

In the background, more is brewing with Lily. She is quite spiteful to Milo. I overheard her in the kitchen, calling him 'thick' and 'stupid' and 'a loser'.

I was shocked. She was never like this. I let Andrea know. Her reply is dismissive. I shouldn't set too much store by it since it's 'just teenage hormones'.

I agree that everything that is happening with Lily is being amplified by hormonal change, but this nasty attitude is something bigger. I can't help but think that it is her mother, behind the scenes, feeding this negativity. I'm not sure why they are targeting Milo, particularly. Maybe he's just an easy target because he is the most vulnerable.

It's beginning to take its toll on me, all this, I have to confess. So many uncertainties. Sending a few emails, however 'no nonsense', doesn't do much to alleviate my helplessness. I need to feel more like I have some degree of control over all this chaos.

Right. Now to get them all up for school. At least I should have some degree of control over *that*.

When I drop Milo at school, I stand at the gate for a while, hanging around long after all the other mums have gone and the last stragglers are safely inside. I'm not sure why I do it. Perhaps I want to make sure that he's truly settled and isn't going to bolt from the grounds because a teacher has confronted him about something unimportant before the day has even begun.

Eventually, I get in the car to drive home. I walk the

pooches, have a coffee, then attack my to-do list at speed and with much more purpose than I could muster first thing this morning. At mid-morning I receive an update from school telling me that 'Milo is struggling'. This seems to happen every day.

By 12.30pm there is another message asking me to collect him. I jump straight into the car, as I've had to do already most days since he supposedly went 'full-time' and get there for 1pm. He's there, in the reception area, waiting for me, looking – as always – like butter wouldn't melt in his mouth.

'What happened?' I ask, wearily.

It's a version of the same response I hear each time. I feel like I could play Milo-Bingo and tick off the phrases. I wish they'd come up with something more imaginative.

'He can't regulate.'

'He shouts and swears at the other children.'

'He was disruptive.'

'He was rude to another child.'

'He wouldn't do as he was told.'

'He refused to listen to the teacher.'

'He wouldn't sit in his chair.'

I always ask if there has been a particular build-up to this behaviour. Can they give me the preamble? 'What happened just before he threw the chair?' I try not to let the weariness I feel make its way into the tone of the question.

Again, little of value is forthcoming.

Today, though, it occurs to me that they always ask me

to collect him shortly after the register has been taken for the afternoon. It strikes me that this is a little convenient. If I collected him *before* lunch, then he'd be marked as absent in the afternoon and that would not make them look good in terms of the whole school attendance record. So, I ask myself, are the school themselves playing the system? It feels to me like they simply don't want him there.

On the way back, I ask Milo a few questions.

'Which teachers do you see first thing in the morning?'

He shrugs and mumbles a name.

'Which ones in the afternoon?'

To Milo, every adult in the school is a teacher, even the ladies in the office. I make a mental note of their names. Later, when Milo is settled in front of *Toy Story*, I do a bit of digging on the school's staff page. I cross-reference the names he has given me and I think I can see a pattern to what's happening.

It's down to the classroom assistants who are there in the afternoons. There are three in the morning, but only one in the afternoon. She looks very young and, if she's by herself, perhaps she can't manage Milo. It could be as simple as that. The school needs to show that he is attending but, due to staffing ratios to children, they obviously have too many children with needs and not enough staff to work with them.

I know that budgets are tight across all schools. The money within local authorities to fund these children is almost non-existent. What would I do if I was the headteacher? Mrs Seymour seems like a nice woman – with an impossible remit.

They know I work from home, so exploit that and get me to bring him back. I'm being played as the easy option. How did it get to this level of manipulation? When did life become this crazy?

I receive a text-message response from Colin, asking how Milo is getting on. I give a brief summary. I'm startled when he writes back:

I'm not surprised. It's always been like this.

Next, Colin tells me that he first tried to get Milo an EHCP when he was five years old.

I am stunned.

Milo's referral was very thin and he still hasn't got a social worker, I tell him.

Colin texts straight back, *What? I was under the impression that he does have one.*

I ask him what he means.

When I wanted to speak to the manager a month ago about the contact arrangement the manager said that the new social worker was Gabrielle and she would be in touch.

I am staggered by this news.

But so far I haven't heard a thing his next message says.

Can we chat again? I ask Colin.

Just call me when you need to. Probably easier than long text messages. Evenings are best as I work during the day.

I apologise, as I realise that it's day time and he is probably working.

He assures me that all is fine. Talking to me is a pleasant distraction while he's on his lunch break.

I email Milo's social work manager straight away, copying in Kendi. Time is moving on and I have so much to do. I'm cross, and it comes across in my terse tone.

To all it may concern,

I understand that Milo has a new social worker and that she is called Gabrielle. I am a little annoyed because I have been messaging you, as his manager, for a month without knowing that Gabrielle existed. Please can we arrange for Milo to meet with his social worker at the earliest possible date.

Regards, Louise.

I drop 'kind' from the sign-off because I don't feel kind right now.

I get a call from Kendi within a few minutes.

'Louise, how are you?'

I explain that there is this mysterious social worker called Gabrielle who has, apparently, been in post for at least a month and has not contacted me. Kendi sounds as confused as me. I realise that I have been merely dancing around a system that slams doors in my face one after the other.

Milo needs a social worker and I need a break.

But it takes another three days before the manager gets back to me.

She is unsure how I know this and can I tell her precisely where I have acquired this information?

It immediately sounds passive aggressive and weird to me. She isn't denying it. So there is a social worker but we are not going to be told? Her comment also feels like she is pulling rank. I wonder if this will create more problems because I have the information and she doesn't know how. If I say 'Colin' he might be in trouble. What sort of living hell is this sector? I should be able to talk like a normal human being but know it's all layers of micro and macro management. Milo needs a social worker. It is as simple as that. What is their problem?

It's an extremely unsettling and unsatisfactory exchange. Kendi speaks to the manager because, evidently, I am too stupid as a foster carer to have a big, grown-up conversation. The upshot is that Gabrielle is currently on sick leave and we'll be informed when she returns.

I'll be on sick leave soon at this rate. Except that I won't be paid and I will still have to look after Milo.

And then, just when I think that it can't get any worse, it does.

XV

It's Kendi who is the bringer of terrible news.

'I'm so sorry Louise. I didn't want to do this over the phone and I don't know how to say this without causing you pain. But Lily's mum has made a complaint about you in relation to Milo.'

'Excuse me, what?'

I put the coffee cup back down on the table, conscious that my hand is shaking too much to hold it.

'I know it isn't the truth, but she is claiming that you are not giving Lily the attention she needs because you are too preoccupied with Milo. Lily is feeling hurt and left out as a result.'

He looks down at his notes. 'Your neglect of her is-,' he pauses to clear his throat, '-is making her feel anxious and depressed.'

I need to scream!

But that will achieve nothing at all.

Kendi suggests one-to-one time with Lily, taking her out

for lunch and shopping. He's probably right, but after the way I've been treated I think cash rewarding a child who is being rude and dismissive because her mother (who happens to hate me) thinks I'm not doing a good enough job just doesn't work for me.

'I'll think about it.'

'This will all blow over, Louise. You just have to stay strong.'

Easier bloody said than done. But overnight, I manage to coach myself into a state of more rational thinking.

This is necessary, because Lloyd can't think rationally at all. He's too busy swearing and stress-rearranging his desk at speed as he hears the news.

I didn't tell him yesterday because I wanted a peaceful evening. I genuinely do not know how to explain this set of feelings. How does a mother who, let us not forget, had her child placed in care by the courts, and has then been quite happy getting on with her own life while allowing us to raise her daughter, suddenly turn on us quite so viciously.

I know why. It's because she has met this bloke she wants to impress and, to do so, she is manipulating Lily.

It would be cruel of me to remind Lily about all the occasions over the years when her mother has promised something and let her down, not turned up, forgotten her birthday.

Now she has the audacity to make a complaint about us, mainly me, because we are looking after a seven-year-old boy. Somehow, in her warped world, she thinks that it's not fair and I'm giving Milo too much attention? We have looked after maybe a dozen different children alongside Lily while she's been with us. Why Milo?

Lloyd is not taking this well at all. Neither am I, but I ask him to fume in a whispering voice. His anger matches my own, but we can't lose our cool. I no longer trust or feel safe around Lily and I don't want her to report back to her mum that we are upset. That will mean that she's won. Won what, exactly, I'm not too sure.

I leave Lloyd to boil in his office and take many deep breaths as I walk into the kitchen. Only to find Lily sitting at the table eating from the giant strawberry family yoghurt pot that was meant to go on the pudding I'm making later. She sucks the spoon and double dips, licks the spoon once more with a smirk before plunging it back into the pot and pushing it into the centre of the table. Then she gets up and pushes the chair back in very deliberately, so that it scrapes along the floor, another thing she knows I hate. She doesn't say a word.

I look and see that she has taken about a third of the pot, but now no one else can eat it. She knows that she should put it away, too. She is doing all of this to wind me up, then tell her mum when I react so that her mum can add more complaints to the list of my crimes.

So, instead of reacting with a reprimand, I smile.

'All right, Sweetheart?' I ask.

She ignores me and walks out of the kitchen.

This really feels like mind games. I'm on the losing side in a weird war that I never knew we were in until a few hours ago.

It sounds dramatic, but since the complaint from her mum, that's exactly how I feel: as though it's war and I need to find a defensive strategy.

Lloyd can't help but come into the kitchen. He makes a coffee, huffing and puffing as he does so. The coffee machine is picking up on his anger and grinds the beans very loudly. While it brews, a wave of humour and mischief comes over me. Lloyd retrieves his cup from the machine just as I jump into a standing position. Tilting forward at the waist, I put my hands on my hips and make a Maori Haka war face. Then I stick my tongue out and do my best impression of Dotty's Chihuahua eyes.

It works. Lloyd spurts out his coffee and laughs. I continue to do my version of Haka moves around the kitchen, to find Lily standing by the door staring at us in disbelief. I turn and face her and jump up and down, repeating my moves.

She walks away mumbling something that sounds remarkably like, 'fucking mental.'

I smile and wonder precisely how this will be reported back to her mum. Even funnier to think about is how her mum will try to convert my theatre into a complaint. Lloyd is still laughing as Lily's footsteps thud back up the stairs.

Fortunately, perhaps, Milo doesn't see my show. The bigger boys catch a glimpse but are so used to me and my antics that they don't bat an eyelid. I resume a more 'normal' Louise face and go to find Milo. I discover him in his bedroom, lining up the box of matchbox cars I've given him to play with and making brrrm-brrrm sounds.

What's the difference? I say to myself. We're both just playing pretend: Milo with his toys and me with my made up haka and all the 'games' I'm having to play with Lily at the moment.

'Hello, Milo,' I say, and ask him what he's up to today. He talks me through the different cars and tells me what their names are. His language has come on a good deal since he's been here, probably because we all talk to him. Well, apart from Lily, but then she doesn't really talk to anyone at the moment. That starts me off thinking about Lily again.

I can't deny that the fact Lily's social worker has raised her mum's complaint concerns me greatly. If I'm honest, my initial fight-or-flight reaction is to serve notice and remove Lily from our home. After all, that seems to be what she wants.

But that's hurt and rage talking. I'm a mother who has had her heart stamped on. And we all know that if we serve notice, the unavoidable outcome will be to invite mountains of stress and anger into the house.

Moreover, I have to think about Lily herself in all of this. She is (legally) still a child, though her tighter, shorter clothing – that must be coming from somewhere else, and I think I guess where – would suggest that she is much older.

This is the same Lily who, not so long ago, felt unsafe

when she walked through town and was cat-called by dodgy men. Now she looks like she wouldn't bat an eyelid at being wolf-whistled. It's hard to believe that they are one and the same person. If I didn't know better, I'd say we had a completely different child.

I pause to draw on my memories as a child, remembering how quickly my friends and I moved through different fashions and styles. It is natural to want to try out different looks. I tell myself that, but I'm not convinced.

The day settles down and I take the opportunity, while there is at least a moment of calm in the household, to undertake a bit of research. I have been keeping a record of my observations of Milo.

One is that he has put on quite a bit of weight. I keep an eye on his food intake and, since the worms, he has not been as ravenous. He eats well and likes all the things children like. He really likes baked potatoes and cheesy beans. He also loves pizza and chicken nuggets and chips. He adores a McDonald's. He does eat sweets but has begun to enjoy fruit. The boys have been great at encouraging him to eat grapes and strawberries. So I'm not sure why he's putting on quite so *much* weight. His diet isn't bad.

But it is the Lily situation which interrupts me once again. I hear her coming down the stairs and, when I put my head around the door, she's clearly ready to go out. Except that she hasn't said where she is going or who with. I hear the door go and dart into Lloyd's study.

'Where do you think she's going?'

Lloyd looks back at me, then grabs his car keys and shoots out the back to get his car. 'I'll find out.'

Fifteen minutes later he is back. 'Tell me what her mum looks like. Can you remember?'

My heart sinks. 'Well, it's been years since I last saw her. But back then she was what I would have called a 'tracksuit-but-no-exercise' kind of woman. Her hair was dyed blonde I think, probably box-dyed because it looked dry and frizzy.'

Lloyd shows me his phone. 'Is that her?' I get my glasses and peer at the image on his screen. It's a picture of a woman in her thirties standing outside the passenger side of a grey Mercedes, talking to Lily. I can see a man sitting in the driver's seat. This woman has long brown hair with blonde streaks at the front around her face. She's wearing a short rah-rah skirt and a pale blue hoodie. Although the hair's different now, I look at the face and see a resemblance to Lily which leaves me in no doubt that it is, indeed, her mum.

Phone contact is one thing, but unsupervised in-person contact like this? It feels a bit like what it must be like to discover that your partner is cheating on you. I can see from the surrounds that the car is parked in the next road. So, we now know what's going on.

Lloyd says, 'Let's email this over to Kendi and the social worker.'

'I don't think so. The complaint will only trigger some

kind of meeting, so let's keep our powder dry. And well done for the good detective work.'

'Thanks.'

I ask why it took 15 minutes if they were only in the next road.

'I actually followed them towards the motorway, because I wanted to know what direction they were travelling in.'

He shows me other pictures, too. There's one of Lily's mum with her arm around her and Lily smiling. Although the images feel like a betrayal, they also remind me that I am, after all, just the foster carer. I must move on and stop myself from being sad about Lily. There's also a natural moving apart during the teenage years, even between children and birth parents. It was always going to happen.

I return to my observations and research once more, with renewed focus. I can only solve one thing at a time. I have made copious notes about weight, but I try not to focus on Milo's weight gain, even though I don't fully understand it.

Other general observations include the fact that he has poor balance. When we played *Simon Says* in the kitchen the other day, Jackson and Vincent joined in. Milo could not stand on one leg and struggled on two when he put both hands on his head. I wonder whether there is an underlying reason for that. I'm still waiting to get his eyes tested. I resolve to take him into Specsavers to start with. I've waited for weeks for the paediatrician to get back to me with an appointment.

Next I turn my attention to the school situation. It's very clear to me that the staff at the school only seem to focus on what really amounts to about 10 minutes of the day's behaviour struggles. That clouds everything. They don't use the time or resources that they *do* have available to try to fix it. They just get rid of him as soon as he steps out of line. I don't see much actual 'support' for him in what they're doing. They seem to just want him out of the way.

If I'm honest, I don't think a mainstream setting is the right place for him. But, without an EHCP, that's all that is on offer. The school admin team are not fussing about Milo being on roll any more. They can show he is there in the morning and perhaps, now, have created a paperwork trail to show that he is struggling.

I'm still not sure what it is that he does while he's there to upset everyone so much, and nobody can really explain it to me. 'Struggling' is the best I get. He finds it difficult to 'regulate' and 'manage emotions'. He certainly can have outbursts of anger. To me, that seems like it might be borne of frustration. Lily has become quite good at winding him up to get a rise out of him. The other day he kicked her. No doubt that will be added to the ever-growing list of complaints from Lily's mum.

I look back over all the notes that I've made each time the school has rung to ask me to collect Milo. A few times they've reported that he doesn't listen or 'struggles' (that word again!) 'to respond to instructions'. I must admit that sounds a little familiar. I've definitely seen some of that myself. So what could be causing that?

It occurs to me that it's worth ruling out whether or not he has a hearing problem. I go upstairs to his room where he is now lying down on the floor, dribbling bubbles from the side of his mouth. He can't see me and he is totally engrossed in his private world. The perfect opportunity to conduct a little test. I call his name.

He does not respond.

I go a bit closer and call his name once more.

Again, he ignores me. I move to within a metre of him and say his name in a normal speaking voice.

He remains oblivious.

I stay where I am and turn up my volume.

Finally, he looks around to see me, slightly startled and clearly having only just heard.

Bingo. That's it!

XVI

My list of observations, that I'm now mentally referring to as 'symptoms' grows.

Poor balance.

An inability to regulate emotions.

Unexplained weight gain.

And now I've got fairly good evidence of some kind of hearing problem. As soon as I start researching all of my observations, all roads lead back to FASD. There's no getting away from it. Foetal Alcohol Spectrum Disorder. It must be. And it breaks my heart. Not just that Milo has it, but that no one else has put all of this together and recognised it. He's been let down. The referral said hardly anything. These are all important bits of information. I'm still letting him down and I hate that feeling.

I also wonder when the last time was that Milo actually saw his parents. Poor boy. He must be missing them. He's meant to be in the 'care system'. Why don't people bloody well care? Our government doesn't care. How can it? Where is the support for all the SEND children? Our prisons are full to capacity and so many young people inside have ADHD, autism or FASD.

It's unfair. I'm becoming angry. I reach a point where I know that I need to stop this for a bit and go and do something calming.

I put a load of washing on and watch it go around. There we have it: low-cost mindfulness. But it's Monday morning. The day isn't going to get itself ready. Well, perhaps the day is, but the Allen household won't without some direct intervention.

I start the round of wake-up calls and let the morning chaos ensue for an hour and a half.

Soon enough I say goodbye to the children, who all head in the same direction but do not speak to each other en route in case someone from their year sees them talking to a sibling and thinks they're soft.

Lily sort of smiles at me on departure, which feels like progress. Or it would, if there wasn't a meeting about her later today. I wonder if she knows. I've been keeping out of her way as much as possible.

It's incredible how swiftly a meeting is called when a complaint has been made about us. I'm still waiting for a social worker for Milo, as Gabrielle is on long-term sick leave. (Maybe she passed out when she saw her case load.) I still haven't got a paediatric appointment and the school has not only managed to *not* request an educational psychologist, they are talking about not being able to keep Milo there as they can't manage his needs. But hey, why worry about any of that when you can quickly call a meeting to patronise a pair of overworked foster carers?

The meeting takes place online in the morning, while Milo is at school. I ignore texts and messages from the school asking me to collect him. To be honest, if they won't teach him, they can offer a bit of childcare while I deal with this situation.

I make two coffees. Lloyd and I sit at his large computer screen, ready to be patronised. Lily's social worker isn't there, but the manager is. A man in his forties with large glasses. He introduces himself but I don't hear his name because he reminds me too much of Brains from *Thunderbirds*. I can tell by Lloyd's demeanour that he is thinking the same. How funny. Kendi is there, wearing black and looking very cool and aloof, until he smiles, and then he looks utterly approachable once more. There is someone from the LADO team, the Local Authority Designated Officer responsible for coordinating responses to concerns.

My blood is up but I stay calm. I have printed off the picture of Lily and her mum getting into the car in the next road. I would never have thought that, back when we first had that lovely idea to become foster carers, we'd ever have to resort to this level of survival mode.

The manager opens the meeting, thanking all of us for attending. As if we had a choice about it. He lays out the premise of why we are here today which, If I am honest, makes me feel like walking out already. The whole tone of his introduction means that he is already presuming we've done something wrong.

Next, the LADO introduces herself. 'But I'm only here to observe today,' she explains, smiling as though this is some kind of TV gameshow.

Observe. My arse!

Hasn't she got anything better to do?

I am fully aware that she has. There must be way more serious issues to be dealing with than the fact that I am fostering two children at the moment and one isn't entirely happy about it.

Brains asks us how we are.

I smile in my best tired air-hostess way.

'And how are you managing with Milo?' he follows up.

Oh dear. I think I want to punch him.

Lloyd says, 'Yes, well, thank you. All good.'

Then Brains asks us what a normal day looks like.

'This is foster care. We aren't sure what you mean by normal?' I chip in. 'Perhaps you could give me an example?'

Brains quietens down after that.

I'm starting to enjoy myself. I read Kendi's face on screen. I detect the slight twitch and curling up at the corners of his mouth. I know him. If he smiles he will go onto full beam. He is trying to keep it cool.

'Let's move on shall we? Kendi, how would you describe Lloyd and Louise's fostering style?' Brains asks.

I am glad this is taking place remotely. Otherwise I really would be tempted to punch him, I swear!

Kendi does the full Kendi. 'Lloyd and Louise are excellent, therapeutic carers who truly understand children. They live in a home that is clean and beautiful and full of love.' He delivers his words with his trademark smile.

'Thank you, Kendi,' I say, feeling a little emotional at his description.

Brains next asks how Lily is.

'Fine, thanks. What do you want to know?'

I'm caught off guard by his next remark. 'I can see that you are quite aggressive, Louise. Are you angry about something?'

I don't have much 'tired air-hostess' smile left to give and say nothing.

Lloyd jumps in, 'May I ask why we are here?'

'Well. Lily's mum, Kerry, has kept a record of how you speak to Lily.'

'What form does that record take,' I ask, finding my voice again.

'She has anecdotal evidence,' Brains smiles.

'Can you be more specific?' I ask.

He clears his throat and peers forward, evidently reading something from his screen.

'Kerry says that Lily said that you tell her off and raise your voice.'

She says, she said. This is worse than a playground spat. I ask him if he has a recording.

'No.'

'And if you did, I would suggest that that would be an invasion of privacy in my own home, don't you?'

Kendi is staring at Brains. He looks cross; not an emotion I associate with Kendi. He makes an O shape with his lips which I haven't seen him do before. It must be his angry face.

And I'm running out of patience here. Not that I had a lot before this conversation began.

'I'm sorry,' I say, in that classic British polite way people use when they mean precisely the opposite. 'Could I just clarify the aim and objectives of this meeting?'

Brains says that he needs to understand what has been going on for Lily. 'We are obliged to take Kerry's concerns seriously.'

When the managers in children's social care are sucking up to the birth family, it's because they're scared about something. Maybe they've identified a legal flaw. Or perhaps Kerry herself has spotted one and has threatened a legal claim. This strikes me as a classic ploy to shift the blame and attention away from them.

'Right. So you have told us what amounts to just some hearsay, via a child in care's mum, but you do not have any evidence?'

'Anecdotal,' Brains says, though he's less convincing this time.

'And, might I ask, what do you know about Kerry's involvement with Lily?'

'Well, we are currently considering arranging more contact, since Kerry has asked to spend more time with Lily. Now that she is older, she can spend time alone with her mum, and this is something we are working towards.'

Lloyd takes his turn to serve now. 'And have you agreed for Kerry to have free contact time with Lily?'

The LADO lady returns. 'This is something that is being looked into.'

Lloyd holds up the printout and says, 'I think you're a bit late.'

They all lean in, including Kendi, and squint.

Game, set and match.

It's wonderful to watch. There is no plan B, other than to end the meeting quickly so that they can cut short how stupid they look.

It doesn't take long for Brains to say, 'We really appreciate your time today, Louise and Lloyd, and we will update our files and forward our thoughts to you, Kendi.'

'If we can be included in the conversations, please? We would like to know what your plans are from here,' I deliver a parting shot.

'That was over quite quickly.' Lloyd and I look at each other.

'Too right.'

A second later the phone rings.

'Hello, Louise, it's Kendi. I imagine they are probably feeling a bit stupid,' he says.

'Which may not be a good thing. I didn't really want to get on the wrong side of a manager with a dented ego,' I counter.

This little mess will come back to bite, I have no doubt.

XVII

Sometimes you get a feeling in the pit of your stomach that something bad is going to happen. Now, I'm not the kind of person who sits back and waits for that something bad to happen. If I was near a volcano that made a noise, I would be the first packed up, in the car, and on the motorway out of there. And I've felt this oppressive doom ever since that weird meeting with Lily's social worker manager and the person from the LADO team whose name I have already forgotten. That's not me being useless or rude, it's survival. Gone are the days when someone was in a role long enough to actually get to know their name, what they did, and what they stood for.

It's the same with GPs. I never know who I am going to see. On any form where a box asks me to put 'GP's name', I used to write the name of an actual doctor who knew me, but now I write the name of a building – because hardly anyone stays. There is almost no consistency in any of our lives – and certainly not in healthcare or social care. I wonder whether this was engineered so that we would end up paying privately for care, or if it's designed to keep us unsettled so we are easier to control? Perhaps I'm overthinking it. It's probably just the cumulative effect of years of incompetence and the wrong people, with the wrong hearts and the wrong experience, in key roles.

But Kerry will not like the fact that we are onto her. And meanwhile, I have the more pressing issue of Milo.

Milo is not having his needs met at school. That *is* a fact. Quite a lot of that has to do with the small detail that most of the time he is not *at* school. They have sent him home again.

I find myself in that hideous position of being a foster carer who, despite stating quite categorically from the start that we can only look after school-age children, due to the nature of us both working full time, has subsequently been manoeuvred into a form of homeschooling. The fact that Lloyd and I both work from home is irrelevant in this equation. And, actually, so is our request for 'school age'. Foster carers were seen to be cherry-picking – though in real life this translates to making sensible choices about what age of child they could look after – and the powers that be made it a blanket 0-18 yrs. But foster carers still make the choices based on the referrals that come in via our emails, and I chose a school-age child. Milo has been at home all day every day this week, and I can't see a way to get him back into school while they are being obstructive.

I am angry with the school, but I also get it. They are

firefighting every day with no resources. This whole system needs a reset. I'm done with being told it's too expensive or complicated. Would British Aerospace say that? Or any other large corporation that dealt with humans as their core business? I don't believe they would.

Once again, I find myself stressed by trying to balance a foster child's needs with my employment needs. Despite what any official who represents fostering might say, the allowances are rubbish and woefully out of date, so we have to top them up with other income streams. And now I also have the issue of what to do with Milo – at home all day in the winter. The local authority seems to have no recognition of their own policy of paying £60 per day for day care.

I desperately want to meet up with Colin and talk to him properly about Milo's current and past situation, but that is proving incredibly difficult. No fault of Colin's, but the fact that I simply can't leave Milo with anyone. No one else will look after him. It's always chaos, and his reputation precedes him. This whole situation is intense and exhausting.

I have to watch Lily and her desire to wind Milo up.

I saw her filming him, but when I asked her to delete the video she denied it. I still love Lily and keep hoping that this horrible time will pass. I look at her when she is relaxed and herself, not acting out a part, and see the girl I once knew.

The next best thing is to try to arrange a Zoom call with Colin. It won't be the same as meeting him in person, but my hands are tied. Only it's not as simple as that. Before the

Zoom, Lloyd has to have a call with Colin and explain how to set it up.

I don't think Colin is that much older than us, but if your work does not require much technology then why would you use it? I only use what I need to and have almost no interest beyond that – which is a reason why foster carers need to be younger. Some kind of tech savvy is required to look after children. If the average age of a foster carer is 60 years, that leaves plenty of scope for predators to access children via tech. But, until they pay foster carers properly and our younger people can rely on it as an income, I seriously worry that foster carers will, literally, die out.

In preparation for the meeting with Colin, I've organised the usual round of meal deals to keep the children quiet. Lloyd has carved out an hour away from clients. I bring in two coffees and a plate of very indulgent cookies from the posh bit of the biscuit section. The door is closed, animals booted out, and off we go!

It goes like this:

Me: 'Hi, Colin, it's lovely to see you again. Thank you so much for doing this.'

Colin: *Smiles and gesticulates. There is no sound.*

Lloyd: 'Ah. You need to unmute yourself, Colin. It's the button at the bottom.'

Colin: 'Oh, there we go. Is that better? Can you hear me now?'

Me: 'Yes, we can hear you now. I was saying that we're really grateful to you for doing this.'

Colin: 'It's no problem at all, Louise, and it's nice to meet you, Lloyd, or see your face, at least. We got there in the end. I've managed to avoid Zoom so far, but actually it looks fine. I'm just a stubborn old technophobe.'

Me: 'Did Lloyd explain that we can't leave Milo at the moment? There's a good chance he might come flying through the door at any time.'

Lloyd: 'But we're hoping that he'll be fine for a while. I've set up a train set for him. He seems to like that.'

Me: 'Colin, when we received Milo's referral, it seemed suspiciously thin, if I'm honest with you. Actually, we declined Milo's referral a few times for that reason and then kept seeing his name. I began to wonder what could be so wrong with a seven-year-old boy that he kept on being rejected.'

Colin: 'That's upsetting to know, Louise. He's a good boy, but he's had some tough things to deal with in his life. I'm glad you took him. I knew you were all right when we met.'

Lloyd: 'We're thinking that it's time we knew a little bit more about those tough things he has had to deal with, Colin, if that's ok? So, first question. Do you know anything about the previous foster carers who looked after him?'

Me: 'Yes, that's something else that doesn't seem to add up.'

Colin: 'I met Michelle in contact once. She seemed a

nice enough lady, but her husband had just left her, I think, so she was a bit of a mess. I was worried that she could barely cope with her own life, let alone look after Milo, so that was a worrying time.'

Me: 'That explains the sandwiches.'

Colin: 'Sandwiches?'

Me: 'Oh, nothing. Were there any carers before Michelle?'

Colin: 'You mean, you don't know?'

Me: 'Know what?'

Colin: 'Before Michelle, he was with this old couple. And when I say old, I don't mean my sort of old, I mean in their eighties. They were nice enough, too, but the house was disgusting. I went there to drop off Milo's Christmas presents. I didn't go all the way in, but what I saw unnerved me. It didn't seem safe or hygienic. They looked like hoarders. I saw a programme about hoarders once…'

Me: 'We've actually looked after children who have been taken away from hoarders and put into the care system. How did they end up placing Milo there? That's ridiculous!'

Lloyd: 'You think you've heard it all, then you hear more.'

Me: 'So can we go back a bit from there? I know that it might seem like we're prying, but we've got so little to go on as we try to help Milo. So, do you remember exactly when Milo went into care?'

Colin: 'Now, let's get this right. It would have been

about two years ago now. Where to begin? My son, Jacky, has epilepsy, has done ever since he was a child. It was serious. Always worried about him, I did. His mum did, too. But you see, we split up when Jacky was three years old and his brother was five.'

Me: 'Oh, I'm so sorry.'

Colin: 'Jacky was the baby and it was a sad time. But I had to work. I was a fireman and on my days off I was a taxi driver. So I wasn't around enough while they were growing up, if I'm honest.'

Me: 'You have to do what you have to.'

Colin: 'Well, it was the usual story. Jacky got involved with a bad crowd at school, then as he got older he began to stay out and eventually moved out. I knew he was doing drugs and that was terrifying. All the drugs caused more seizures, and he was taking them on top of his meds for the epilepsy. I was always waiting for the call to say he was dead. But we couldn't stop him. Nothing we said had any effect. Then he met Sally, Milo's mum. She was a nice enough girl, she worked in a care home in the beginning. But then she was sacked for stealing drugs from the locked cabinet. She was bang to rights: caught on CCTV doing it. Not long after, she came into the family way with Milo.'

Me: 'Did she have other children?'

Colin: 'No, not that I know of. I mean, I met her parents and nothing was said.'

Me: 'What's Jacky doing now?'

Colin: 'Oh, that lad. He's been in and out of rehab. Things change for a week and then he goes back to the drugs. He's never been strong. He always was easily led, and so he always gets dragged back.'

Me: 'And what's happened to Sally?'

Colin: 'She took an overdose and died two years ago, when Milo was five. So that's when they took Milo away. I didn't know that had happened until afterwards. I didn't even know I was a grandad until social services came looking for Jacky.'

Lloyd: 'That's absolutely tragic. I'm so sorry. We've never been told this.'

Colin: 'Jacky couldn't look after him, of course. That wouldn't have been safe. He's never been able to look after himself, let alone another human being. So, Milo was in the hands of the care system.'

Me: 'The poor boy! He must be grieving. Does he know about his mum?'

Colin: 'No. The social worker at the time, Laura, her name was. Have you met her?'

We shake our heads.

Colin: 'Well, she was a piece of work if ever there was one. Forgive me, but she was a right stuck-up bitch. She turned up in a bloody great 4x4, then kept on telling me that her kids were at private school and her husband was in finance. She was about as much use as a chocolate teapot.'

Me: 'So, does Milo actually know his mum is dead?'

Colin: 'No, or at least, not as far as I know. Because this Laura, in her infinite wisdom, said that I wasn't to tell him in case he got upset.'

Me: 'He must be so confused about where she is.'

Lloyd: 'Wow. So what did she think not telling him and waiting would do to him?'

Colin: 'I just did what I was told. I mean, these people are supposed to be the experts.'

Me: 'Did he start school? The school he's at now has effectively rejected him. They've said that they don't have enough support because he didn't start with an EHCP. I suspect they couldn't face it. We have no information about his previous schools, so it would be a help if you could…'

Colin: *Reaches down and pulls up three carrier bags of paperwork.* 'They are bloody shits, excuse my French. I've been fighting to get Milo into school and get an EHCP since he first went into care, when he was living with the old couple who didn't know what an EHCP was. I mean, *I* didn't know what an EH bloody CP was then, but I do now, after all this lot.'

Me: 'So those are all documents relating to Milo and his education?'

Colin: 'Yup, myself and my partner started creating an evidence trail to help Milo and it's been a bloody nightmare. I know it was too little, too late. I know I should have been involved before then. But I've been trying to fight for him. Until you two came along, he didn't seem to have anyone on his side.'

Lloyd: 'I've got to say, I'm slightly struggling to make sense of all this. Especially since Milo still hasn't got a social worker.'

Colin: 'His social worker is Gabrielle. But when I called to speak to her I heard she was on long-term sick.'

Me: 'That's expensive. The department will have to find someone else to cover her.'

Suddenly there is a bang at the door. It's Lily. We thought she was out, so it's nice to know she's home. She has Milo by the scruff of his neck. 'He threw Douglas off the sofa.' She drags him back out and slams the door.

Colin: 'Looks like you might need to go.'

Lloyd: 'Yes, we should intervene there. But let's stay in touch. By the way, I've got to ask. Are you a Ska fan?'

Colin: *Chuckling.* 'You could say that. Yes. I'm a massive fan. At last count I had over 300 singles and something in the region of 1,000 albums.'

Lloyd: 'Oh, wow, I like…'

Me: 'Right, I'll leave you two to talk. I'd better go and see Douglas.'

Colin: 'I hope he's all right. Is he another foster child?'

Me: 'No, he's a dog. Bye for now.'

Colin: 'Let's stay in touch. Call me if you need me, Louise. And thank you for everything you're doing.'

And I exit stage left, leaving the two old musos to it. I hear 'Rudy' being discussed on my way out. I head straight to the sitting room, only to find Douglas curled up asleep on the armchair. Dotty is on the sofa and all looks well. There's no sign of Lily or Milo downstairs. I wonder where they could have gone.

I actually feel quite tense. I know it's mostly in my head, but Lily has had such a different vibe about her lately that it's hard to not think dark thoughts. I half-walk, half-run up the stairs and head directly to Milo's room where, to my surprise and delight, Lily and Milo are sitting on the floor playing snap together with a pack of Lily's old cards.

Wow, this is just about the last thing I expected. It's also wonderful!

'Um. Douglas? Is Douglas okay?'

Lily says that Douglas jumped straight onto the chair and Dotty didn't move.

'So no one hurt him?'

It's only just dawning on me that when Lily came into Lloyd's office she was actually *playing* and, judging by Milo's grin, he was, too.

I'm so relieved, I sit on the end of Milo's bed and stare into space for a few moments in a stunned silence. Then I remember all the woe in Milo's life, and all the grief he still has to suffer.

'Would either of you like something to drink?'

They both report that they are full and fine, thank you.

I go back downstairs and into Lloyd's office. I'm smiling as I sit down to re-join the conversation, but can see that Colin and Lloyd are too deep in as they discuss the relative merits of Jamaica Ska over London Ska. As far as I'm concerned, they might as well be talking about tax returns or cricket. I'm already bored and there's no room in this conversation for me.

There is one more surprise in store at bedtime. For months now, Lily has had her phone surgically attached to her, reacting defensively if anyone went near it. Because her mum bought her the super-duper iPhone-whatever-number, we lost our rights and ability to take it off her. But tonight, she brings the phone down voluntarily and puts it on the shelf with the rest of the family's devices. She doesn't even put it on charge. After everyone has gone to bed, I can still hear it pinging. When I go downstairs and check it. I see multiple notifications of messages from 'Mumsie'. I can't – and wouldn't – read the messages, but it's interesting to see what amounts to a bombardment.

I'm so fed up with the incessant noise that I wrap it in tea towels and put it in the conservatory under a cushion.

I go in and say, 'Goodnight,' to Lily, and thank her for playing so nicely with Milo.

'Are you all right?' I ask, curious to see if she has any kind of separation anxiety from not being on her phone.

'I just need a break from Mum,' she says, and looks away…

XVIII

Today I wake up feeling more rested. I don't know why, but sometimes you wake up and feel great – and today is one of those days. Maybe it's because Milo and Lily played together. Perhaps it was Lily's confession that she needs a break from her mum. Wherever it has come from, I have energy.

The house is even running as it should: the children are all where they should be and Milo has managed to get himself dressed. Well, after a fashion. He has fresh clothes aplenty, but has mistaken one of his pyjama tops for a day top and has odd socks on, heels twisted round to the front of his feet. The ensemble is endearing, and I'm not going to ruin his day with matters as trivial as correct clothing; instead, I congratulate him on his good work and decide that I'll just pop his windbreaker over the top when we go out.

I have a plan. Last night I was wondering what we could do today. I feel like doing something new, something different. Or at least something different as far as Milo is concerned.

I decide that, if we leave at 9.30am and get petrol and

a treat or two for Milo en route, we will be at my secret destination by 11.30am. I've already booked the tickets online and saved 30%. I pack a little bag of 'all sorts of things' that I take away when I take younger children out. First-aid essentials including antiseptic cream, toys and activities, tissues, a bottle of water, snacks. I let Milo know that we are off for a magical adventure.

'Where?' His eyes are wide and he claps his hands together. 'Where we going?'

I know that it's always a risk with children in care to offer up surprises. You never know whether they've been on the receiving end of a 'horrible' surprise from someone who is nasty. But I think I have gauged Milo to be okay with the idea of a surprise.

'It's a good kind of surprise,' I say. 'You're going to have to wait and see.'

He moans, 'Nooo! I want know now! Peeese Louise, I want know now.'

Although his language has come on in leaps and bounds, Milo still has a habit of mispronouncing things and missing out little words in his utterances, as though he hasn't quite learnt the rules yet.

I do my best Mary Poppins impersonation and say, 'Oh, supercalifragilisticexpialidocious! Even though the sound of it is something quite atrocious, if you say it loud enough, you'll always sound precocious! Supercalifragilisticexpialidocious!'

He giggles loudly.

I pat him on the head and do a little dance as we gather our coats. 'Just in case it rains.'

I hold Milo's hand and lead him first to Lloyd's office. Lloyd swizzles around in his desk chair.

'Goodbye, Lloyd,' I say, with a theatrical flourish. 'We're off on an adventure.'

Milo backs me up with a, 'Lod, we're going on a denture.'

Lloyd smiles and plays along. 'Now, you be good you two, I know what you're like.'

Milo loves this and giggles into his hand, beaming his little head off. Here we are, partners in crime. Lloyd had printed out our entrance tickets because my printer, as always, has run out of ink. It doesn't take a lot. I think I hate my printer. It's actually Lloyd's. He swapped with me to help because his was easier to use. Or so he said. But not as far as I'm concerned. I still manage to have a breakdown, resort to pressing random buttons and regularly end up swearing at it. It's actually quite therapeutic. I like to use it to take out other frustrations, too.

I make sure Milo can't see the logo by folding over the top of the sheet, not that he would, realistically, know what it was. I kiss Lloyd on the cheek and Milo giggles again. He takes hold of my hand once more as we exit the house and head to my car.

I straighten out the bumper seat in the back and strap Milo in after he makes a few clumsy attempts himself to bash the seatbelt in the vague direction of the clip. I strap myself in, say, 'Clunk-click,' which Milo repeats, and turn on the engine.

I put in the postcode for our location and rootle around in the glovebox for the Kidz Bop CD. We're soon on our way. Milo is so happy. I check him in the mirror and see that he is grinning and chatting to his teddies, who have already been released from his little red rucksack. I love moments like this. I feel totally warm inside.

I can't find the words to describe them and really do them justice. They are like drops of pure magic that I know won't last. Which, on one level, is a good thing. If they did last they'd be the norm and go unnoticed – but I live for these moments. Nothing makes me happier than to have the privilege of catching glimpses of a child totally absorbed in the moment, unfettered by any awareness of others. It's very special. I love it. And, whatever happens, today I will be satisfied with this passing moment.

We travel along the motorway for a bit and I manage to resist Starbucks and Costa, though they call to me. I take our exit and keep driving along the dual carriageway.

'I need pee pee,' Milo announces, after an hour or so into the journey.

'I'll pull over.'

'Pee-pee, pee-pee,' he chants over and over until I find a suitable place to stop. I pull into the entrance of a fruit-picking farm for Milo to do his business. He gets out of the car, clutching his groin. He dances about until I find a nice bush for him to wee behind. He thinks it's hilarious when he turns around spraying a perfect arc over the bushes.

When he's done, we are back in the car and on our way once more.

I check the sat-nav clock. Another 20 minutes to go. I'm grateful that we're not too far away now. It's keeping him happy, but I have to confess I'm finding his music to be a little on the repetitive side. Behind the clouds, the sun has made an appearance, and there's even the glimpse of some blue sky. The sunshine makes the car feel warm. I hope it lasts; the forecast did say showers when I checked, but perhaps we'll be lucky.

We drive through a series of small, pretty villages and come out the other side along a country lane. It looks like we're heading into nowhere, until we see a massive sign that reads, 'Welcome to Bert's Farm'. There's a painting of an old farmer with hay in his mouth smiling like a Disney character, surrounded by piglets, lambs, chickens and geese, and a bright red tractor in the background.

'Milo, we're here.'

He looks up and bounces in his seat.

'Wow,' he says, gazing up at the sign. We drive into the car park, where there are more wooded cutouts of animals smiling. It is actually quite lovely. Two old fellas appear, dressed in high-vis over thick, pale plaid shirts. They also sport green ties, big green wellies and green peaked caps. They smile as they direct us to a parking spot. As I help Milo out of the car, they offer five-star VIP treatment to Milo.

'Are you the sort of young man who likes animals?' one asks, with a cheery grin.

Milo nods, wide-eyed.

'Well, if the young gentlemen would like to follow us this way, I think some wonderful adventures await.'

Milo is made-up by the attention. These two are so friendly and jolly; what a great marketing touch. They show us where to go and offer Milo some stickers for his pyjama top.

'Very smart. Good choice,' one of the faux-farmers winks.

Milo tries to wink back and ends up performing an exaggerated blink. I have a very happy boy.

He holds my hand and stands still, waiting patiently as I try to wrap his rucksack around him, only releasing my hand from his for a second to allow me to secure the straps onto his shoulders; then he has his hand straight back in mine, but it's for excitement as much as reassurance. It also has the added advantage of stopping him from running off. I don't think he'd do that now, but in the first few days of being with us I couldn't trust him not to dash in the wrong direction or dart in front of a car.

We stand in line at the entrance, where we catch glimpses of animals in pens beyond the barriers. I offer my printout to the lady behind the counter who, like her carpark colleagues, is also wearing a cloth peak cap. She smiles at Milo and offers him a little badge of Bert's face. I pin it on his top next to the stickers. They certainly know how to make children feel welcome here: Milo is already walking taller with all the fuss.

We follow the arrows in the direction designed to give us

a tour. I clock the toilets and café. I suggest that Milo goes to the loo as I need it too, then grab us a hot drink. Coffee for me and a hot chocolate for him. It's still impossible for him to eat or drink without looking like it's the first time he's tried to do it, and he ends up with a little ring of chocolate around his top lip. Now, though, he doesn't mind me wiping it away for him. He'd have run in the opposite direction if I tried to do that when he first arrived with us.

Hands washed, and refreshed by our drinks, we head on our way round the farm. His face lights up with excitement when we meet our first show-stoppers, the baby goats. Milo gets so much exercise as he runs around and back again, then hops about from foot to foot, desperate to show me things. He's like Dotty or Douglas on a walk, covering quadruple the distance that I do.

I stand holding his bag and coat and look into the distance where I see a field of reindeer. I find this sight fascinating and by the time I turn back Milo is halfway up a rope on a climbing wall in the adventure play, laughing and doing a loud impersonation of a monkey.

He is having such fun, which means that I am, too.

My tummy tells me it's lunch time. I didn't bring a picnic today. Given that there are only two of us rather than six, I don't mind treating us to the restaurant food. They know their audience, so it's basically a menu of sandwiches, chips, sausage rolls and crisps. I get in line with a tray and ask Milo what he wants.

He frowns as he thinks very carefully about his decision. He is being so good, I can't quite believe it. Normally he – and most children, to be fair – would be asking for more. Perhaps demanding chocolate, cakes or sweets. He points at a cheese sandwich, surprise surprise, but seems quite content with that. It's as if somehow he might understand that he's having a good day and may appreciate what he has. At least temporarily.

After lunch, we stand in the very long line for the petting shed. I hear rumours of piglets, rabbits and guinea pigs brought in to be held by excited visitors. I feel a sense of wholesome wellbeing. A convoy of children and adults in wheelchairs pulls up behind us, all waiting to hold an animal. I hold Milo's hand and he keeps looking up at me, making the best excited faces I think I've ever seen. There are twin girls a bit younger than him in front of him who keep turning around to look at him. He pretends not to see them, but I know he has and he drops his head with shyness.

As with everything else in this place, the queue is well-managed; a green-capped helper chats to us while we're waiting, and soon it's our turn. We are welcomed into a barn that has been arranged like an ancient amphitheatre, except the seating is hay bales rather than stone. We sit down next to grandparents with two young grandchildren who are super-excited. Their anticipation isn't helped by grandad, who is so excited for them. I think he might be about to burst. Granny does better and keeps it all under control. I like watching people, especially when it's this wonderful little slice of humanity. I'm surrounded by happy people and I feel even more energised by them.

Once we're all seated, in come trollies, wheeled by more Green Caps. A trolley of guinea pigs, one of rabbits, chicks, and piglets follow one another in rapid succession. They look like babies being pushed through the maternity unit in cribs. We are each given a little blanket to put on our laps by a number of healthy-looking rosy-cheeked junior workers in blue polo shirts with Bert's Farm embroidered near their hearts. I wonder how long it takes to earn a plaid shirt. One young lass says to us, 'What animal would you like to cuddle?'

Milo beams at me, then looks at her without speaking. Then he looks back at me as if seeking permission.

'Choose, Milo, go on.'

He points at a long-haired guinea pig that makes me think of Donald Trump. I think about making a joke with the polo-shirted girl, then choose to say nothing. I don't want to bring politics or fake news into this barn of joy.

She looks at me expectantly and I say, 'A piglet, please.'

She wanders off to lift out the piglet and places it on my lap. I feel a little awkward about this as I've never cuddled a piglet before and I'm not entirely sure how much cuddling this one will stand for. Still, there's something about baby animals that is so winsome. I'm also anxious to keep an eye on Milo to make sure he doesn't hurt his guinea pig in any way. I don't *think* he would, but all that destruction in the early days has left a residual caution. I needn't have worried.

When I look at Milo he is radiating love for this little creature, being very, very gentle and stroking it with a single finger.

The sheer joy that fills the barn is incredible. I look around and see nothing but smiles in every direction. Grandpa and Grandma next to me are taking photographs of their granddaughter with a tiny chick in her hand. It strikes me that the corporate world should abandon their slides and pool table and introduce an animal petting zone at major conferences. Imagine CEOs in suits snuggling up to lop-eared rabbits. The world might be a nicer place.

Our time is up and our beautiful furry friends are gently taken from our grasp. I feel quite tearful as I say goodbye to the little piggy whom I have been happily chatting away to for about 20 minutes. Piglets are quite affectionate, I've decided. Milo hands over the guinea pig without a fuss, but then asks to hold a mouse. That boy has charm, I think, as the girl wastes no time in picking one out for him. The mouse runs around his arm and across his shoulders making him giggle, but does not leave him. Milo and the mouse are genuinely playing. I find this extraordinary and fascinating. I think I might want to live in this barn.

On the way out we walk through the gift shop. These places seem to be designed so that you can't escape without going through it. Today, though, I don't mind. I give Milo £10 and we spend some time trying to work out if he wants to get several little things or a big thing. He falls in love with a guinea pig soft toy; happily one that bears less resemblance to Mr Trump. He also falls in love with a little piggy toy. He convinces me that he needs both, even though that takes him over the £10. But look at his face! How can I resist? I fold and buy both, along with some chocolate animals for the others. It's 4pm and I head off back down the country lane. Milo has guinea and piggy on his lap.

He is about as happy as I've ever seen him.

Days like this make it all worthwhile.

The forecast rain never arrived, and on our way home the autumnal sun is low and bright, shining into the car. So much so that I find myself reaching down to the little area by the gear stick to get my sunglasses. I have my right hand on the steering wheel and, just for a split second, Milo suddenly puts his hands around my head onto my eyes. The car veers off the road and up a curb. Thank God, I mean thank *all* the gods, of which there are, apparently, over 3,000, that there was not a cyclist or pedestrian in the way or I might have killed them! I do not co-regulate this time. I shout, 'Milo, sit back down NOW!'

I make sure the car is safe. I get out and open the passenger door to lean across Milo, pull down the seatbelt and click it back in. He must have unclipped it while I was driving. I look at him, without any therapeutic, co-regulating or trauma awareness and say, loudly and firmly, 'You nearly killed us, you silly little boy.'

I think he's as shaken up as I am.

What a horrible end to an otherwise perfect day.

XIX

In the post the next morning is an envelope from the hospital. Finally we have been given an appointment with the paediatrician. It's not for another four months' time, but still, it's a start. At least we have a letter, a date and a time. Still nothing from the dentist. I send my weekly *Hello, are there any updates?* message to the dental surgery. They will be sick of me soon enough.

There is a flood warning for later. I must say, since the town came out in protest about the repeated flooding of the area, the multiple agencies who are responsible for the maintenance of the highways, drains and pipes, and the farmers who are responsible for clearing the ditches, have all stepped up. They soon got fed up with cross residents posting on Facebook about how rubbish they are, and things have been better for a while. It's annoying that we'll have to think about flood defences once more.

But one small win is that I have managed to get an appointment with Specsavers this week, so we can at least get an overview of what's going on with Milo's vision. Another small win that's weird and unexpected is a continuation of the better humour from Lily. The ceasefire between her and Milo seems to have held up. I'd even go as far as to say that Lily and Milo have begun to bond. She says 'hello' to him when he comes down for breakfast and offers him biscuits from the tin unprompted. While I'm not sure that he needs any more biscuits, and certainly not with his breakfast, given that he seems to be putting on quite a bit of timber lately, it's a welcome change in dynamic.

It transpires, though, that Andrea, Lily's social worker, has now gone on sick leave, just as this elusive Gabrielle has. I plug away with Kendi to see what's happening about Milo's replacement social worker, but there's no news. It's a very frightening sign when so many social workers are sick. Because these days we are with an independent fostering agency, as opposed to a local authority, we have two children from two different local authorities. Because of the crisis in diminishing foster carers it's almost the norm to be fostering a child from another county, or even a different part of the country. The knock-on effect of that is that the social workers and their managers are less likely to know each other, and they all seem to do things differently. That bit isn't helpful. There are national 'minimum' standards (never national maximum standards, that would be good), and they all aspire to the minimum. Often they don't even make that minimum as far as I can see. Also, I've begun to notice that each local authority seems to have a different interpretation of what the national minimum standards are. Not even each local authority, but sometimes within a single authority. Often, there doesn't seem to be consistency from department to department, office to office, worker to worker.

The nicer atmosphere in the house continues for the next few days. Lily appears to have stepped down from her high horse. Her phone still keeps pinging away and distracting her from the real world, but at least some of the old Lily is back. Perhaps she's starting to settle back into some kind of equilibrium again after the complicated reintroduction to her mum. Perhaps, as Kendi suggested, she has come to realise on which side her bread is buttered.

On Thursday, Milo and I head into town for his appointment at the optician's. While we're booking in at the reception desk, I notice that they advertise hearing aids, so I ask if they do hearing tests as well.

They do, and given that it's not too busy, midweek in the daytime, we can book in for one straight after they have done the eye test. Milo is fantastically behaved for about 10 minutes, then the ants in his pants are released. He starts giggling and will no longer sit still or answer the optician's questions about what he can and can't see, but descends into giggling and silliness. The optician is patient, but I have to take Milo for a quick walk around town to reset before we can get the results and then go through for the hearing test.

The eye test suggests that Milo has some cloudy spots in

the focusing part of the eye. He has small, weak nerves in both eyes, and his right eye is lazy. Treatment can begin with a patch to make him use the weaker eye. Milo is delighted by the pirate look.

His hearing test comes back with a diagnosis of 'intermittent conductive hearing loss'. Apparently, this can be caused by a build-up of earwax, or there might be something lodged in both ears – which is more unlikely. Or there could have been damage to the bone from prenatal experiences, which is consistent with the kind of damage that drugs and alcohol during pregnancy might cause. I hope for the earwax, but I know where my money lies, given what we now know from Colin about the sad history of Milo's mother. I'm not surprised, and it's good to have my suspicions confirmed. I was right. He really can't hear. All those anti-social signals he was sending at school and at home were not his fault. It all gives me a great deal to think about.

We have another contact meeting with Colin.

He's dressed as before, though today he sports a thin tie instead of the braces with his big boots and his pork pie hat. I feel as if I've been transported back to the 1980s again. I feel a pang of nostalgia for those faraway times.

Milo rushes up to him once more and Colin sweeps him up in his arms.

'I wear your hat?' Milo asks.

'Of course you can, little fella,' Colin says and pops it on Milo's head. It's too big for him and falls forward over his eyes, but Milo giggles as if this is the most fun it's possible to have. Colin has bought more toys, again carefully chosen. One is a 'den' kit, a simple design of interlocking pieces that clip together to build a fort or a castle. It just needs a sheet or blanket thrown over the top – but he's thought of that, too, and has a camouflage-patterned blanket in his bag to complete the den.

While he plays with his grandson, Colin tells me a little more about his history.

How he used to be in a soul band and performed in local pubs.

'We had a great laugh in those days and, I'm not going to lie, I liked the attention from the girls that came with being in a band. I loved to party. I also rode a Vespa and had a fishtail mod coat. Do you remember them?'

I do indeed, and I think I quite like the sound of the young Colin!

'But that's enough about me. We're here to concentrate on this little fella!' Colin says. He gets down on all fours like a giant bear and takes Milo on a tour of the room on his back, Milo giggling all the while.

'I thought about becoming a social worker once, myself, you know,' he tells me later on, when Milo is pushing a train around the tracks they've built together. 'A long time ago! Years before I joined the fire service.'

He tells me how he had a girlfriend who was training to be one.

Milo's Story

'I was claiming benefits while I looked for employment and thought about possible careers. I was selling the Red Star and the Socialist Worker paper in the town every lunchtime outside the civic centre in the Guildhall.'

He used to see a beautiful Indian girl go into the building each day and began to time his presence to match when she might come out for lunch time. He asked her out and they began a relationship. She was on her work placement in the children's social care department, next to housing.

'My parents were Scottish. My dad was a factory worker and my mum worked in the NHS, so I was very aware of the issues affecting the disadvantaged.'

He was a keen socialist and wanted a better society.

Don't we all, Colin, don't we all.

The hour is soon up, and I am fascinated by his story. It's totally irregular, but he asks if we've got time for a coffee after. It's a mild enough day for the beginning of November. The sky is a pale blue with weak sunshine, and Milo has his big coat.

We go to the park and he treats us to coffees from the kiosk. He tells me more while Milo is on the climbing frame.

At the same time he met the Indian girl – the love of his life, as he describes her – an ex-girlfriend, whom he had split up with a while ago, announced that she was eight months pregnant. 'I was quite a naughty boy back then,' he says, with a wink. 'But that was my wake-up call and I did the right thing.'

The right thing was that he went to support his ex-girlfriend. They moved in together and he got himself a factory job like his dad. Another baby quickly followed the first.

'We stayed together for a few years. But it was difficult. We weren't in love, and I felt as if my life had disappeared.'

He tells me how he would smile when he saw his friends out in the street and he was stuck pushing a buggy.

'Done too much, much too young! I'm married with a kid when I should be having fun.'

He recites The Specials ruefully.

Eventually, the little unhappy family broke up and, for a period of time, Colin found himself back at his parents' house while his sons stayed with his ex.

'I chose the fire service and loved it. I was still only in my mid-twenties and I felt I was finally claiming some of my life back,' he smiles as he remembers.

'I saw as much of my sons as I could. Which wasn't enough. Jacky went a bit off the rails and my ex couldn't cope with him and threw him out. I should have done more to help then.'

This memory is evidently quite painful for him. The smile is gone.

'The older lad was OK. He went off and got himself an apprenticeship in a tax firm. He became an accountant and did all right. But Jacky – well. His life began to fall apart, I suppose. The epilepsy was a big thing. But he took too many drugs and he was in and out of relationships. It wouldn't surprise me if he had another kid somewhere that I don't know about yet. But then he met Sally, and she was into the gear big time. She's the one who really messed him up. Milo was born, and a whole new load of problems began. They stayed together for a bit, history repeating itself in a way, I suppose. And then – well, then it went tragically wrong when she took the overdose.'

I nod. We still haven't come to a decision about what to tell Milo about his mother, or when. Or even whether it's our place to.

'Thanks for being so honest.'

He smiles, a little sadly. 'Ah, well. There's been enough lies in this family in the past.'

Back at home after school, the atmosphere in the house still seems reasonably peaceful which, while lovely, is a status that I don't entirely trust at the moment. I have been lulled into a false sense of security before. But I shall take all the calm I can get.

Lily, for once, does not rush straight back out of the door, and instead stays home. Today she's watching telly without her phone by her side again. She is still wearing pretty interesting outfits that I'm certain her mum has got for her, at least judging by the outfit Kerry was wearing in the picture Lloyd took. But she seems a little bit discombobulated.

I don't blame her for taking a break. Especially if she feels that her mum is 'full-on'. I can't disagree, given the amount of texts coming through. A more thoughtful individual wouldn't be texting their child late into the evening, especially not when they had school the next day. Weirdly, when I reflect on it, Kerry's behaviour and its effect on Lily has all the hallmarks of county lines: incessant texting, new expensive clothes and phones, change in behaviour. We've been *there* before with other foster children. But this has nothing to do with county lines drugs' gangs. She's Kerry, and she's Lily's mother.

While everyone is occupied, I decide that I will start to sort out the summer to winter clothes turnover. I've had so little time that the summer clothes are still folded up into piles on the floor. It's November, and I still haven't examined what I need to get out for winter. We're all improvising in in-between clothes. I know that I shrunk my lovely red jumper that I bought last year and I should probably replace it. It made me look more alive than some colours. Purple, for example. I look dreadful in that – any shade of it.

I'm looking for some things in particular – I know I've got some thick cord dresses with pockets, somewhere. It makes me mind less about the changing of the seasons. Oh, how I love pockets. But, even without pockets, it feels lovely to have even a tiny bit of time to myself. The trouble with relaxing, for me, is that I need to find a way to wind down, or I sort of go a bit bonkers. I drift around, wondering why I went into a room. To get what, exactly? I go to make a coffee, put it down and forget about it. I hope it's my way of letting go rather than dementia creeping in. Lloyd appears and stands in the bedroom doorway as I pack the piles of summer clothes into laundry zip bags. He doesn't say anything, just keeps staring at the bags.

'What's wrong?'

'Kerry has made another complaint.'

'She's done *what*?'

I'm up and out of the bedroom, my knees aching from kneeling down too long. I follow Lloyd downstairs to his office. There it is in an email, signed off by Brains, the social worker manager. We've been called to an emergency disruption meeting.

I pull my phone out of my pocket and call Kendi who answers straight away.

'Louise, yes, I just saw it. Do you know what all this is about?'

I say that I have no idea and start to tell him how calm Lily is and how much more peaceful the whole house has been for the last few days.

He says he knows, because I haven't contacted him.

I read the email again. 'It says that Lily's mother has made a complaint, but there's nothing here about what it might be. To call a disruption meeting is either because they love drama, or they have nothing better to do.'

'I'll see if I can find out anything more.'

'There's a third explanation,' I say. 'It could just be spite because of Lloyd showing Brains the picture of Kerry and Lily getting into the car. It did make him look like a prat.'

Or something terrible has happened, but we missed it. I don't say this to Kendi. I'm also starting to wonder if Kerry could be angry because Lily seems to have pulled back a bit. What Brains and his team conveniently seem to have forgotten is that there was a reason why Lily was put in care and taken *away* from her mother. I seem to remember conversations about Kerry's mental health, her anger, violence and addictions. Has she changed?

I feel my face harden as I say to Kendi, 'What else are you going to do?'

'Louise, you know I will be there, and I will question everything.'

Lloyd is not like me. He did not grow up in care and finds threats to our family and sanity at the hands of social services very stressful. I reach out and touch his arm. 'It will be all right, hold your nerve.'

I can tell by his face that he is not convinced.

XX

What do I do? The meeting of disruption is in two days' time, which gives me two days to feel dreadful. And only two days to create a game plan. But, as far as I know we haven't done anything wrong. It would just be helpful to have the heads-up about what exactly we might be being accused of this time.

What I do decide, is that we say nothing to Lily or the other children. We give this, whatever it is, no oxygen.

In the evening, I notice that Lily's phone is back on the shelf. I'm proud of her. It's good to see that she's taking control. I'm proud of anyone when they let go of their devices and free themselves from that awful digital toxicity that draws people in. Me? I just block people, without question, without hesitation. I'm quite Marie Kondo about my online life. If they do not spark joy, then they go. And my real life: if people are rude, I do not see them again. It's as simple as that. I ignore any emotional guilt-tripping. Someone being unpleasant might be going through a tough time, that's unfortunate, but they're not going to take out that tough time on me, thank you very much. I listen to my instincts. If someone appears to have bad intentions, I do not welcome them in.

We have a two-pronged attack at play here as far as I'm concerned. Brains strikes me as being trivial and emotionally immature. He is a manager, and some of that hierarchical power appears to have gone to his head. I suspect he has been licking his wounds after our last encounter and is seeking some sort of petty revenge. It seems to happen so often: that inappropriate people are given power beyond their capabilities. Brains is one flank of this ambush. But we also have Kerry, already known for her poor judgement and behaviours. If she was taking her parental responsibility seriously, she would not have parked in another road to see her daughter on the sly. All that deceit takes its toll on Lily. For the last few years in our household, she's been raised to be honest. I also know, from experience, that having two mothers is a nightmare.

Lily will have seen that 'bitching' about me and my family and life makes Kerry happy, so because she doesn't actually know her mum that well, she will be doing everything she can to develop that relationship, making her mum happy by giving her what she wants to hear. No matter that it might be at the cost of all that she has. It's an attachment built for the wrong reasons, and that's always dangerous. Lily has been used as a kind of toxic messenger for her mother.

I, on the other hand, become an easy target. It's just like in the case of separated parents, where one has the lion's share of care and responsibility while the other can be the fun, part-time parent at weekends.

It's certainly not that I'm a saint in this situation. Far from it. But the fact of the matter is that I do not need to know anything about Kerry, I do not need 'feeding'..

I think Lily is tired of being torn in two, and probably feeling trapped.

I can imagine that her mum has promised her the world. New house, new room, holidays, new life, everything she could ever want. Poor Lily must be in a complete spin.

I have enjoyed the relative calm of the last few days and I need to keep things that way. I also need to keep Lloyd calm.

Over time, I've learnt that when Lloyd is under threat, stressed, or worried, he talks about how much everything costs. It's rather tedious – because I don't want to know – but I'm aware that it's his way of coping. Part of it, I'm sure, is a kind of validation that he makes a material significance to these foster children's lives as well as an emotional one. If we didn't financially prop up the placements, these children would have a meagre existence. I brace myself for the reckoning.

After dinner, once the children have disappeared off up to their rooms, he goes through all the things that we have done and paid for above the fostering allowance for Lily. It's long. The holidays abroad, the trips to London (which are so expensive we probably *should* have gone abroad instead), the clothes, the horse riding lessons, the new bedroom furniture. On and on and on. It starts to feel endless and it goes into the thousands. I put my hand on the table and say, 'Stop.'

It's a kind of torture that is being self-inflicted. 'This isn't achieving anything. It will only make you even more vulnerable. Leave it. What does it matter? It's only money. You can't take it with you and the boys will be all right. We have food in the cupboards, which these days is more than a lot of people.'

Lloyd looks down at his hands and nods.

The irony, in the midst of all this, is that Milo has really settled down. Part of me thinks that the removal from school was fortuitous. Maybe this is what he needed, no school, no more new faces. Who would have thought? It's wonderful, but has taken its toll on my earnings and time, which I am trying to ignore in the midst of all the focus on money right now.

I sit on the sofa after clearing up the kitchen and Milo hovers in the room for a bit. Then he plumps himself down next to me and leans in. I think I could cry my eyes out. Especially when I think about all the trauma he's already been through in his little life, and the grief to come that he doesn't fully know about. It's all too sad. I put my arm around him and kiss his head.

'Hello, gorgeous boy, you okay?'

He pops his head up and smiles and says, 'I'm sucking my thumb.'

Now, to most people, that's no big deal, but for Milo that's a fully formed sentence and he knows it. I look at this boy beam.

The bigger boys are totally oblivious to the impending meeting of doom, and that's good because their lack of awareness is helping to keep everything normal. Lily appears back downstairs, too. Not to spy, or say nasty things, but because she wants a hug.

I pull her in and she sits on the other side of me. She is back in her Lily clothes, looking natural and relaxed. All the heavy make-up has been left off and she looks much younger. I put my arm around both children and stare at the blank TV screen. No one has put anything on, but we don't need anything. We all need to be still and close. We all need *this*.

XXI

The day of the meeting arrives. Lloyd takes Milo swimming first thing in the morning. The swimming has been going really well and we've noticed that it is one thing that does seem to tire him out. Lloyd has grown very fond of Milo. Still, I always had a feeling, even before Milo arrived, that he would be visiting, not staying. There was too much missing from his referral, and the situation of still not having a social worker is a massive issue.

The latest update on that is that Gabrielle is due back in two weeks. I bet her manager and colleagues love her; they would have had to pick up the slack in her absence.

Lloyd walks through the back door with wet hair. Milo troops in cheerfully behind him. He also has wet hair, but his is sticking up. He has lovely rosy cheeks from the exertion.

'I'm hungry,' is his opening gambit. As Milo walks through the kitchen, he crashes into a chair. I no longer think this is deliberate. I think he didn't see it. It's not wanton destruction, when I think back to some of the things he has broken and destroyed, it's visual impairment and Developmental Co-ordination Disorder (DCD), a common symptom of FASD, which makes him appear to move clumsily.

Lloyd looks across the room to me, then says in a whisper, 'His torso is chunky but his legs are thin.'

I frown, because I've been worried about his weight for a couple of weeks now. Then Lloyd asks, 'What was Colin like when you met him?'

I explain that he looked well-proportioned to me. I can say that as an artist. 'But I didn't really look too hard because I was bedazzled by his chunky gold sovereign jewellery and white shirt and red braces. I hadn't seen a rude boy up close for years. I was busy trying to take it all in.'

Lloyd shakes his head. 'Maybe it comes from his mother's side, then.'

'Hmm. Did you have a good swim?' I ask, as I put some toast on for Milo. Lloyd asks for a piece too. I feel for Lloyd. He's not the greatest swimmer himself; he splashes when he swims. If I'm there I make faces and tell him to stop splashing. I see people look at him as he inadvertently breaks swimming pool etiquette. His dad was a swimming instructor, a great swimmer, a diver in the navy – but he never taught Lloyd. His dad was on the Parent and Teacher Association at his school and managed to get a new indoor pool built. It was a facility that other schools could use too. Lloyd thinks that his dad was rather busy with the women, and that's why he ignored the fact that his own son couldn't swim. People, eh? As I get older and meet more people, it seems to me that the happy, sound families are in a minority. The rest of us are just at various stages of dysfunction. I put the toast on a plate and call Milo. He crashes back into the kitchen, swerving the chairs this time. Bravo!

Lloyd checks his phone and reminds me that we have the meeting in 10 minutes. Like I needed any reminding. He scoffs his toast, wipes his mouth and makes a black coffee. I decide to refrain from drinking more coffee. That could be dangerous. I settle Milo in front of his modular building set, put on a film and cross my fingers that the swim will have tired him out enough to keep him contained in the sitting room while we are in Lloyd's study for the meeting. I fill up a glass of water and, as I pass the hall mirror, I apply more lipstick. I keep three shades of lipstick on the marble top tucked behind an African mask. They each serve a different purpose. This feels like a 'muted brown' meeting, not red.

In we go. The door is closed, pets are out. We sit side by side as Lloyd presses the link. Good god, there are loads of them. Who are they all? Obviously, there is Brains, and Kendi is there, but so are a bunch of people I have never met before.

Brains welcomes us all and asks us to go around and introduce ourselves. I write down each person's name and role on a pad in front of me. There are 12 people, not including us and there I was under the impression that there was a staff resourcing issue compounded by people being off sick.

We have two teams here, and Lloyd and I are on the rookie team. There are people from the virtual school, an alternative online education provider, plus Lily's actual school, the wellbeing team, and Lily's actual social worker, Andrea, whom we have now not seen or communicated with in ages. On Milo's side we have someone from commissioning, a business support worker, no one from school but someone from their virtual school, and Milo's social worker's manager and someone else. Who they are I haven't a clue. Perhaps no one knows and they're just there for the show. Plus, of course, ever reliable, our supervising social worker, Kendi.

Brains starts the meeting by laying out his reasons for calling it.

'We have received complaints from Lily's mum that she is not happy. She is particularly concerned that you, Louise, have said some cruel things to Lily about her mother.'

This immediately rubs me up the wrong way, as he no doubt intends it to. 'So,' he continues, 'can you explain what *you* think this is about?'

Wham. He's just set-up a kangaroo court. I am too experienced to play his nasty little game. I lean in and say, 'Good morning. Before I say anything, I wonder, Martin, if you could elaborate further.'

The notepad is coming in useful for names.

'Could you also provide any evidence you have to support this complaint?'

I have my pen poised.

'And, may I also ask you, ultimately, what your objectives are here today?'

Kendi leans in. It's amazing how he can demonstrate support, even remotely, through a gesture. I think he felt he should because I did.

It's all got a bit *Judge Judy* and we've only been going a few minutes. Oh, and I've decided I'm going to be Judy.

Kendi says, 'Indeed, Martin. Can you explain where your information has come from?'

Martin, or Brains, pushes his glasses back and says, 'I received an email from Kerry, that is Lily's mother. I had emailed her regarding the printout that Lloyd Allen displayed in our last meeting, the image which showed Kerry and Lily next to her partner's car.'

Everyone else is sitting still. I don't know if this is because they think we are the Wests, or they are wondering why they are there. Everyone has a poker face on, apart from Martin Brains and Kendi. Martin's lips are pursed and Kendi looks on full alert.

'Are you able to offer more detail about what it is I'm supposed to have said?'

'Bear with,' he says, as he squints at his screen. 'Ah, yes. Here we are.' He proceeds to read out a section from her email. 'Lily has repeatedly told me how unhappy she is at the Allens. She reports that ever since Milo arrived in the house nine weeks ago, all they do is run around after him and ignore her.'

My blood is up.

'It goes on,' he says, and clears his throat in a way that feels totally unnecessary to me. 'Louise called Lily a selfish bitch. She shouts at Lily all the time for no reason at all. The Allens don't care about where Lily is when she's out and about. She's had enough of being ignored and wants to leave.'

I watch Kendi. I can see that he is fuming. But he rarely lets that professional demeanour slip. Before anyone says anything naff, I steam in.

'Can we see the screenshots please, or audio recording of these supposed conversations?'

But Martin Brains is angry. 'Louise, can you explain to everyone what you think this is all about?'

I'm fuming. It's hard to keep my cool. It's so unjust! 'I have never said *any* of those things to Lily.'

'But I have to believe her truth, Louise.'

What about my truth?

Kendi says, 'We have to respect that Lily may be feeling some strong emotions. Her mother, also. But it does seem to me that you are forgetting that Louise and Lloyd have provided a stable and loving home for Lily for a number of years. I ask you, Martin, why you believe the emotional anger of a mother who has not lived with her child? Kerry will, no doubt, be feeling many emotions such as guilt and shame. Could it be that she is magnifying Lily's comments or feelings?'

Kendi is as eloquent as ever, but I can't help feeling that Martin is determined to punish me in some way. I'm not sure what for, other than pride. He's getting back at me in numbers because I made him look a little foolish last time.

Martin is insistent. 'Louise, please can you explain what happened and why you said these things.'

It's like he's not even listening to the words I'm saying. I will myself not to feel upset, but I can't help it. I feel bullied and humiliated. I love Lily. I have *never* said anything like that to her. I know I haven't because I have been so bloody careful whenever I talk about Kerry, to avoid this very scenario. How dare they? I am full of emotion and rage. I start to cry and say, 'I can't do this.'

I push back the chair and leave the meeting and the room.

From the other side of the door I hear Lloyd say, 'Well, thanks for this, Martin. I've never seen Louise this upset before. She's done nothing but love and care for Lily, as if Lily was her own daughter.'

I don't want to hear how he responds to that. I walk away from the door and into the kitchen, where I huff and puff and plonk myself onto a kitchen chair.

Milo walks in and frowns. 'Are you orwight?'

Oh, bless him. I have become very fond of this little

boy and, right now, I don't know what the plan was for that meeting. What is it they are trying to achieve? Do they want to remove Lily? Remove Milo? Or was I just put there to be shamed by Martin?

Sometimes, I ask myself if it is because I write about children that I am unpopular in this world. Other times, I wonder if it is because I was once in care myself and know the system from the inside out. I have found that I sometimes anger professionals for reasons I'm not entirely able to fathom, just by virtue of having been in the position of these children once.

'I'm just feeling a bit sad,' I say to Milo. 'I think a hug would cheer me up.'

Milo obliges by throwing his arms around me and almost knocking me off my chair, which makes me laugh and cheers me instantly.

Then he pats my head and says, 'Don't be sad. It's a happy day, Louise.'

I look at him and make a curious face. He pulls my hand and takes me into the sitting room. He has built a Lego fire engine, almost perfectly.

'Wow, I am so impressed!' I tell him. And I really am. He's right. It is a happy day because his happiness at his achievement takes my mind off the drama still being played out in Lloyd's office.

It's another half an hour before Lloyd comes to find me. He blows out his cheeks. 'Well. That was interesting.'

'I disagree. That was horrendous.'

'Coffee?'

'Wine.'

I ask what happened.

'Well, once you left and – actually, are you all right by the way?'

'Yes, I am. I am finding joy in Milo's fire engine.'

Lloyd nods, as if that's perfectly normal.

'After you left, Kendi managed to shut Martin down. He was actually quite angry in a Kendi sort of way, and totally defensive of you.'

'Good old Kendi!'

'Then, a bit later, Martin said that Kerry has made a complaint about me, too.'

'Go on then, surprise me.'

'She's complained about me photographing her.'

I look suitably exasperated.

'Louise, what do I do for a living?'

'Well, last time I checked, you were a graphic designer.'

'Yes, and one of my jobs is to oversee all the picture editing. I would never have shown Martin that photograph in the first place if I hadn't known the law. If you take a picture of an adult or child on public land, such as a path or road, you do not need consent.' He pauses. 'There's no law to prevent you from taking photographs in a public place.'

'Right.'

'Right. Which means that f***ing idiot should have

checked that before he started accusing me of things. And, I mean, why were there so many people there? What was he trying to do?'

'I've been asking myself the same question. I'm not sure.'

'No, well, whatever it was, I don't think it went down too well. But you know what this lot are like: they close ranks and protect each other, despite what they actually think.'

'I can make a good guess at what happened, Lloyd. Martin was using Kerry as an excuse to unsettle us and to rock Milo's placement. He, or they, are worried about something, I bet you. They probably don't want Lily to go back to Kerry, but they're scared of her, too, so pushing Milo out would probably keep her happy. What a load of crap. The fact that there are two local authorities is not helping. Because Lily was here first, they will claim rights over her placement to Milo's.'

'But we've always fostered multiple children.'

'Through the same local authority.'

'And what about our rights, eh?'

'Well, as we know only too well, Lloyd, foster carers don't have any.'

I wonder if this will calm down or become worse. Either way, I am not sitting back and waiting for the unknown.

I have an idea.

XXII

By the next morning, I am feeling much calmer. Actually, not 'much' calmer; that might be overstating the case somewhat. But I have a little more perspective.

I call Colin.

I put him on speaker phone in Lloyd's office while Vincent and Milo are seriously involved in a game. I explain to Colin what happened yesterday, and what we think they are trying to do. I express all my concerns about Milo being forced out and having to go into another foster placement. As I say it, I cry. I'm feeling very emotional about all of this. Why are the children never at the top of the agenda?

And why do people play games? Why can't everyone just be honest about what's going on? It makes me feel enraged and devastated at the same time.

Colin says, 'Well, I'm sitting here with Leah, my partner. My fiancée, actually. We've been talking a lot and we'd already decided that, when the time was right, we'd like to take Milo in. Given everything you've said, that might be rather sooner than we were expecting. We've been exploring what's involved in becoming kinship carers.'

'Are you sure about this?'

'He's my grandson, after all. We want him out of danger and away from this bloody system. It's done nothing for him.'

I take quiet umbrage at that. *We have done something for him!* Or, at least, we've been trying our hardest to do everything we can for him. I almost say it, but in many ways, Colin is right. Milo *has* been let down by the system. I know it's not a personal attack.

'Why didn't you step up before now?'

'I was working full time when Milo went into care. It all came as such a shock. I was dealing with a lot. And actually, do you know what? I wasn't even asked, originally.'

'Family options are usually explored first.'

'Maybe they thought I was too old. I was single. I don't know. Then, later, when I did put myself forward, I wasn't considered suitable. But I messed things up when Jacky was young. I messed things up over and over again with Jacky, and I'll never forgive myself for it. It's time to right the wrongs of the past, as much as I can.'

I no longer care about being awkward. I say. 'Is there something, anything, that might prevent you from taking him this time?'

I've already fought so hard for Milo, I feel like a tigress. I will not let any further harm happen to this child.

'No, Louise, absolutely nothing. Leah and I are planning

on getting married next year. It would be good to have a page boy.'

We all laugh.

This is the solution that Milo needs, I'm sure of it, but we need a strategy to make it happen. I'm already thinking ahead.

'Right. This could really work. What I suggest is that you contact the manager straight away, and make your intentions known. Copy in Gabrielle, though who knows if she'll ever come back. Talk to them about having Milo. They will have worked out what Lily's lot are doing and, with the current crisis in fostering meaning there are not enough foster carers, they may be pleased with the idea. It's a solution that should appeal.'

Part of the reason it's likely to appeal is that it's a much cheaper option for a local authority than long-term foster care, but I don't say that.

'There will be checks and interviews. They like to look in your pants drawer, if you know what I mean.'

Leah screeches with laughter at that.

'But what will really go in your favour is the relationship you already have with Milo. He obviously adores you! It's a big part of the viability assessment.'

The plan is hatched. We will keep Milo safe for as long as we can before Lily's social work team force him out. And, if he moves to his grandad's, he will not be in foster care at all – which means we will not need to ask stupid Martin's permission to see him or have them over for tea when we choose.

For now though, Lloyd and I say nothing about it to anyone at our end, not even Kendi. He is genuinely upset and has, with his manager, made a formal complaint in reply to Kerry's nonsense – well not that, but Martin's handling of it. He recorded the meeting, the clever man.

'It was outrageous. Martin should never have questioned you like that in front of all those people. That was incredibly unprofessional. I was not the only person to think that. I could tell that others thought so too.'

'I'm afraid that it was a little unprofessional of me to walk out the way I did. I'm sorry about that.'

Kendi reassures me that I was not behaving unprofessionally as far as he was concerned, and it was my right to leave. 'You were being bullied and humiliated and he was ignoring your questions and your side of the story.'

Kerry still keeps submitting complaints about me and the family, Kendi explains, 'but now they have to go through me first.' Kendi will be the one to decide if he thinks he should bother us or not. Now, this is what I call proper social work supervision. He has our back and that's all we ever wanted.

Despite the hassle of leaving the local authority to join a family run agency, it has been so worth it. And, even with all this current aggro, we do not regret that decision at all. We feel safe. That seems an odd thing to even say, but how can we foster vulnerable children if we don't feel safe and supported ourselves?

The flow of complaints slows down over the next few weeks. I know that Kendi doesn't tell us everything, and instead he is probably batting things away in the background. Milo and Lily continue to grow towards a kind of truce. So, regardless of what Kerry might be saying, it doesn't seem to be affecting Lily's quality of life too badly.

A happy and unexpected bonus is that Martin disappears off our radar fairly quickly, thank goodness, having found a new post in another county. I may have suppressed a little cheer at the news. Good riddance to – well, I won't say it. So, round and round they go.

Then, after a few weeks of relative stability, we meet Colin and Leah for lunch in a pub near their house. It's a lovely old pub with impossibly blooming hanging baskets at the front. Inside, all its old-world charm and quaintness is emphasised in polished horse brasses, painted beams, and ye olde worlde signage. It's almost overdone to the point of actually no longer being charming.

Milo orders chicken nuggets and chips, and manages to stay in his seat for a good third of the mealtime, which counts as progress.

After the lunch, we pop back to their home. A seventies semi-detached property with a bright red front door that immediately makes me think of Colin's braces. It has a good size garden which they've equipped with a climbing frame.

Milo is delighted and immediately sets about swinging off of different parts of it and performing somersaults from the upper storey. I turn away, trusting that he has enough instinct of self-preservation not to do himself harm, but not particularly wanting to watch. While Milo is busy outside and Leah busies herself making coffees, Colin explains about his latest conversation with his son.

'We visited him in rehab and told him about Milo coming to live with us.'

'He was so happy,' Leah says.

'So happy that he's promising to clean himself up and get a job so that he can be part of Milo's life in the future,' Colin adds.

Leah smiles a tight-lipped smile. 'Yes, love.'

Colin looks down at the floor. 'Well, we'll see.'

It's too early to tell Milo about the future plans, in case anything falls through. He also struggles to manage concepts surrounding time, so it would be difficult to explain why he couldn't come straight away. Nevertheless, Leah and Colin have been busy preparing his room in readiness, under the guise of having a potential sleepover in the future, something that has already been agreed by the managing social worker.

'Would you like to come for a sleepover at our house?'

'Yes! Seepover!' Milo nods eagerly at the prospect.

They've bought him Lego-themed bedding, and have kitted his room out with some books and toys including a box of assorted Meccano, which is something I haven't seen for a while!

Colin looks sheepish. 'It's the sort of thing I should have been doing with Jacky when he was a lad. I can't turn back the clock, but I'm going to get things right with my grandson,' he says.

I know Milo will love it here when the time comes.

At home, we see a much happier Lily. I feel as if we are reaching a balance. Her mum is spending a fortune on her – and show me a teenage girl who doesn't enjoy that! Mostly Pandora jewellery, clothing from JD Sports, tonnes of make-up and new trainers. Most of it sits in the corner of her room unused. None of it is really Lily's thing. But she politely takes it. And knows it's her mum's way of saying that she loves her.

XXIV

It doesn't take long for Colin and Leah to become officially approved as kinship carers. They pass the 'viability assessment' without too much fuss. Essentially, it means that they do not have the equivalent of parental rights, but will look after Milo in agreement with their local authority and Jacky's wishes.

It seems a little harsh and out of sync when Colin and Leah are doing this *because* Jacky has a problem with addiction and responsibility. Kinship is like fostering in many ways, except they will receive even less money, but they will have Milo, and a family will be back together.

We have all been mindful not to speak of this plan in front of the children, especially Lily or any of Lily's social workers. Many's the slip between the cup and the lip, as the saying goes. As it moves towards fruition, Kendi is also quite happy to have professional cloth ears around the subject. He even offers a few suggestions – in a 'hypothetical' way, of course. Kendi is far too wise to jump the gun.

As we get to know each other better, I find both Colin and Leah hugely inspiring and such amazing fun, too. Milo is familiar with Ska music and, because of Leah's West Indian roots and connections, he is also becoming very familiar with reggae, one of my own personal favourite music genres. Leah and I sing Jimmy Cliff songs to each other down the phone. She does make me laugh.

Because of Milo we have gained new friends, whom we now hold dear. That's another one of the joys of fostering when it goes well.

Colin has done some research into the meds that Jacky was taking for years to manage his epilepsy. There is a lot of controversy about a particular drug, and a campaign is mounting against the pharmaceutical company that manufactured it. I don't know the technical stuff, but I do know that Colin has joined a group of parents whose children had taken the medication and have suffered side effects from it. They are campaigning to get it removed and fight for compensation. There is some theory that it could have been passed to Milo during conception. It's a worrying thought that something like this could have affected an unborn child – on top of the non-prescribed drugs that Milo's mother was taking during the pregnancy. I don't know how accurate this is, but Colin is convinced, and animated when he talks about the group. These things are much easier when there is more than one of you.

As a consequence of his findings, I'm able to give the

paediatrician a much fuller account of Milo's background when his appointment finally comes up.

During the appointment, we learn something surprising which starts to explain a great deal.

The paediatrician introduces herself as Patricia. 'Patricia the paediatrician' is quite the mouthful and almost sounds as if it's been made up, but she laughs as she tells us that, even though she must have said the line hundreds of times before. She is a delightful, older lady who has a maternal air that sits above the professional one, and an aura of calm that seems to rub off on Milo. He is able to sit still and allow himself to be examined. She turns the session into a game so that Milo is able to use the stethoscope on her.

She frowns when she learns about the epilepsy drug on top of the maternal history I can provide her with. Coincidentally, it's something she has already been reading about, and she's aware of the controversy surrounding the drug.

Milo is diagnosed with something called Cushing's Syndrome, which may be linked to it. The characteristic symptoms of upper body obesity and weight gain had been masked, by the severe case of worms, which stopped him putting on any weight while they were eating away at him. It's likely, looking back on his fostering history that I now know a little bit more about thanks to Colin, that the ongoing worms infection was from being in a placement with the two very elderly foster carers. They lived like hoarders and were totally unfit to be looking after a young child, being barely able to care for themselves. The worms were most likely left untreated for a significant amount of time, because he was with his other foster carers, Michelle and Andy, for several months after that.

Other symptoms of the syndrome include muscle weakness and difficulties with memory and concentration, all of which Milo seems to suffer with. It explains a lot. Combined with FASD, the poor kid was up against it from the start, even before a turbulent home environment and the tragedy of his mother.

Life seems so unfair sometimes.

Epilogue

Milo runs up to me in the museum, sporting a mini pork pie hat, just like his grandfather.

'Don't you look smart!'

A few months ago, I'd have been worried that Milo might knock over some priceless artefact, but he's learning how to behave in public spaces, and understands the 'rules' a little more when they are communicated to him properly with appropriate awareness of his hearing and visual impairments.

Knowing that Milo's future is set gives me great relief. The more we know him, and the more we know *about* him, the more obvious it is that he should never have been in mainstream education. Given the problems with hearing and vision, it's totally unsurprising that he couldn't cope with school and school couldn't cope with him. Until he gets an EHCP, he's not going to be able to cope in mainstream education. Colin's paperwork may help speed things up in that regard. At least we have evidence going back further than a term, but even so, it could still take ages.

While that happens, Colin and Leah have been busy creating what they are creatively describing as an 'alternative education programme' for him. They've put hours and hours of work into it and are taking it very seriously. They've torn up the rulebook and have begun to organise their lives differently in order to make it happen. They both have part-time day jobs that they've structured to allow them to play tag with each other, which means that someone is always able to be home with Milo: they can take it in turns to do daycare and education. They have a big chart up in the kitchen, colour-coded with who's doing what and when. When they talk me through the detailed plans of this alternative provision, I can tell that they've really considered all angles. They've put so much work in and really thought about finding ways to make education all about engagement. It strikes me as something that should be rolled out across the country.

Of course, Colin is taking care of Milo's musical education.

'And does that have a heavy bias towards Ska and two-tone?' I joke.

Colin is also responsible for what he is terming 'outdoor learning', that is a mixture of Forest School-type initiatives, PE and some cultural excursions and visits – in the local area initially and then further afield. Hence the museum as a meeting point today. They've planned in an outing a week for the whole of the next term.

Today is a 'living history' day at the museum, and Milo

is going to make various potions as part of an organised 'mediaeval apothecary' event. He's excited to get his hands on 'dragon's blood' and other gruesome ingredients. I feel like I want to study this curriculum!

'Leah is going to manage the teaching of core subjects,' Colin explains. 'And I get to do all of this fun stuff.'

They have been thinking about ever more innovative ways that they can 'hide' functional maths and English into their activities, so it's more fun and less 'schoolroom'. The emphasis is on practical learning, but with a view that, when he does eventually go to a school that recognises his needs, Milo will be up to speed. They're armed with resources and have also got in touch with other home-educators in the local area, so that Milo will have the opportunity to meet other children his own age who are in a similar position to him at least once a week, which will help to develop his social skills and prevent him from being isolated.

Milo is a lucky boy.

And one final mystery is solved when, prompted by his grandad, Milo shyly hands me a little piece of paper.

'What's this?'

He dances about from foot to foot.

'Party.'

I see that it is indeed a birthday party invitation.

'Why, thank you, Milo! That's very kind of you to invite me. I'd love to come!'

Nobody, not even Colin, seemed to know when Milo's

birthday was. It wasn't on his referral form and it seems that his birth was never registered originally. Perhaps it's not surprising if both parents were in the throes of drug addiction. It might not have seemed a priority. While Milo happily mixes up some hideous concoctions under the watchful eye of the museum facilitator, Colin explains how he found out. He'd been trying hard to pluck the information from his son.

'It transpires that I'd been paying for a tiny lock-up for my son for years. It was one of those direct debits that goes out every month that I'd forgotten about. In trying to tidy up my finances ready for taking on Milo, I noticed it and went to clear out the lock-up. There were a handful of boxes stacked in a corner, some a little worse for wear, thanks to some sort of rodent that had been chewing away at things. I closed down the storage account and moved the boxes to my attic.'

'Go on! What did you find?'

'I found a pile of Milo's baby things. Among them was a half-started baby book made by Milo's mum.'

He takes the book out and shows me.

'Ah, that's wonderful. At least he has some of her handwriting to remember her by.'

'And look at this.'

He shows me where, at the front, it has Milo's name and, next to the word, 'Born', a date and time: March 12th at 5am.

Milo's Story

Finally!

Like so many others, though, he will perhaps not really begin to understand what has happened to him until he is much older. For most I speak to, it's their 30s and 40s when they put the jigsaw together – and that's when they need the emotional and therapeutic support the most. Up until then, life is mostly spent trying to get on as best they can and doing their best to fit in. At least now he has some stability around him to help him do that when the time comes.

'How's Lily getting on?' Colin asks, having been filled in on some of the drama and complexities of that situation. I tell him about how Lily is still with us and, though it isn't always easy, things have calmed down a little.

For a while, she seemed hell-bent on breaking up the placement through the complaints and accusations that were being hurled at us. The campaign wasn't Lily's though, it was being driven by her mum. It was a little short-sighted. I don't think Kerry really thought through what would happen to Lily if their mission had been successful. Where would Lily go? Would her mum really be able to look after her? So far, she hasn't successfully looked after any of her children. They have all gone into care. The care system takes no prisoners, and it isn't as simple as deciding that she's ready to have them back. There would be an awful lot to prove before that could happen.

There are days when Lily forgets herself and is Lily again, then it shifts back to the contrary teenager. We savour the space in between. Lily's schooling has gone a bit wonky and her teachers who have always been so impressed with Lily's studentship and scholarship are as upset as we are. We're doing our best to get her back on track.

'Perhaps I should bring her on a Milo education day,' I say with a smile.

We say our farewells and Milo turns back to wave at me as I leave the museum.

'Goodbye, little soldier,' I murmur.

Afterword

I cannot state this often enough: Milo's issues are not his fault. We must strive for a kinder way of living which acknowledges this.

Each story I write about – and I deliberately say 'story' rather than 'case' – opens my eyes to new issues and challenges and exposes the gaps and flaws in our system of social care.

Sadly, I've had more experience than I would have liked over the years with FASD. It's a problem on the rise in the UK and across the world. But I'd never heard of Cushing's Syndrome before I met Milo and, thankfully, it is relatively rare. I was repelled by the idea of worms when he first arrived. None of those things were Milo's fault.

His situation was compounded by poor supervision once he arrived in care. The elderly couple from whom he was removed were probably excellent foster carers once, but old age is cruel and, being increasingly incapacitated themselves, led to further neglect of Milo.

Michelle and Andy were the wrong candidates for foster

caring. They entered the system for all the wrong reasons. A financial motive isn't going to lead to the best outcome, and greed has no place in a system of care. They were lured in by promises that never materialised and, in the end, actually sacrificed personal wealth and wellbeing to pursue the ideal. It never could have been a reality – not in the way that they imagined it. At first, they just wanted school age children so Michelle could give up her job at the town hall and spend her time running her perfect new life with a 4x4 to whizz them all to school with their little rucksacks.

Of course, that is not to say that we shouldn't pay foster carers a fairer sum for everything they put in, just that it shouldn't be the only reason for coming forward to help children.

Michelle and Andy's relationship was destroyed by the experience. Michelle was struggling to make ends meet and found dealing with Milo's issues too much to cope with on her own.

I'm happy to report that Milo is now thriving and, I suspect, will continue to do so. He is a lucky boy to have Colin and Leah in his life. Not all children in care have someone willing to take on the huge responsibility of looking after them. Those who have found their way into the care system are often the most vulnerable children in society. Inevitably, that means that they will bring plenty of emotional baggage with them. It takes work to support that level of emotional need. How much work, and exactly what will be needed is mostly unknown at the start. There isn't a handbook for all the situations that will arise.

Colin and Leah love Milo. Of that there is no doubt. That love will see them through. Jacky, Colin's son is much better these days and comes to stay at the house with them, developing the beginnings of a relationship with his son. We can only speculate, but perhaps Jacky learning that it's likely the meds he was on for epilepsy that have led to some of Milo's issues, has somehow given him a kind of wake-up call and enabled him to focus his priorities differently.

None of us have any idea, really, what Cushing's Syndrome will mean for Milo and his future life. It looks likely that Milo's conditions have been compounded by FASD. The list of different challenges he faces is long. Problems with movement, balance, vision, hearing, lack of concentration, the ability to manage his emotions — all are connected to the two diagnoses. Getting any support these days is near impossible. I think that the barriers to obtaining an EHCP and delays in SEND assessment, the lack of enough trained educational psychologists to cope with the current levels of demand, the refusals from local authorities protecting their budgets in the face of national underfunding, all these things will become a national scandal.

Milo, like so many children, was disregarded by society. It's all too easy to get pushed into the wrong places by our broken care system. Schools, with their own budgets overstretched, and managing ever more oppressive curriculum demands, do not have capacity to intervene in the ways that they would want to. Somehow, the picking up of these fragile, painful pieces seems to have become their job. It is not – or, at least, it shouldn't be. Teachers completing PGCE (post-grad certificate in education) courses or entering the profession by undertaking immersive, on-the-job training, do not have the specialist knowledge needed to educate a child with the complexity of needs that Milo has.

The tragedy this causes on an individual level is immense. But it also has wider issues for our society. Youth crime and prison sentences are affected when so many young people seem to present with symptoms that look like ADHD or autism. In the UK, it's estimated that up to half of the adult prison population may be neurodivergent. Sometimes behaviours result from neglect or damage caused by drugs and alcohol – or simply society's inability to understand and accommodate neurodivergence. Without vital support, children with these conditions can be left to grow into awkward, disaffected, vulnerable, socially incompetent young people, who are more likely to fail at school and be disruptive, have mental health problems and substance abuse issues. This, in turn, makes them the perfect target for gangs such as county lines, or other exploiters.

So, what can we do?

It is the job of our society to educate our young people to the dangers of taking prescribed and un-prescribed drugs. I was watching *Annie* the other day, the version made in

2014 with Cameron Diaz, and Quvenzhané Wallis playing Annie. There's a line in it which quite explicitly argues that it's mobile phone companies who rule our world. I would concur but would also add pharmaceutical companies alongside them.

I think governments are scared of them, so we must stand up to them or no one will.

Parenting is hard work and it changes you. Your life becomes 99% about looking after your children and doing right by them. That goes for foster carers, special guardianships, kinship care arrangements and all forms of parenting. Our needs do not come first. We eat last, not first. We need to be more honest about the demands of parenting and move away from anything that sugarcoats the role. Girls are becoming pregnant not because they are bored and are promiscuous as some would think. They may have been coerced, or made poor judgements, or in extreme cases, have been victims of rape.

Often, girls and women who have had adversity in their childhoods and have suffered abuse and neglect learn that mostly, whilst they are pregnant, they receive kind attention from the services. That's a welcome change that feels like nurture. We treat mothers appallingly, but often it's their vulnerability, pain and ignorance that has created so many babies with these problems. It always goes back to education. If young girls and boys truly knew just how much work was involved in raising children, they would think again. I have met young mums who had children because they wanted the same pram as a celebrity.

Give me strength!

Milo's mother was not able to look after herself, let alone a child. Her story is a tragic one that had devastating consequences for her son. There are very few care stories that end up as neatly and as happily as Milo's has. He's one of the lucky ones.

Acknowledgements

The Allen family has been lucky. We have had the privilege and sometimes the terror of sharing our lives with the lives of children and young people who, for whatever reason, cannot live with their families. Some go home, some move on and occasionally some stay with us.

My birth children, Jackson and Vincent, have seen and experienced so much. Sometimes (or 'often' if I am truthful), I have worried that being foster siblings would hurt them. Maybe the sharing of their parents with other children would be too much. Lloyd and I have worked hard to give them, we hope, the attention that we believe they need. But not so much that they feel suspicious or smothered. It has been hard and, as parents, we really do, and have, put the children – all the children – first.

As my sons get older, I no longer have the fears I used to. I see the outcomes of all our experiences and hard work. They are two amazing young men who are aware and emotionally mature. They do not judge and I rarely hear anything negative spoken about others. They are solid and truly themselves. I still worry and turn myself inside out about all of the children, but I am watching my boys grow into good men. So, this time I want to acknowledge my sons Jackson and Vincent, whom I love and admire hugely. I want to say thank you and I wonder if, one day when you are grown and have lives of your own, you will become foster carers?

Thank you to Lloyd whom I have known since I was 18 years old. We have reached that stage in life where one is talking, the other leaves the room and comes back and nothing is said. We just keep talking.

I now have more cats, thanks to Jackson and one of our more recent foster children, under the guise of 'therapy cats'. They certainly make their presence felt while I'm writing. We still have the two best emotional support dogs I could wish for: totally untrained, a little bonkers sometimes, but a huge and important part of our family. Thank you to my canine pals, Douglas and Dotty.

Thank you to my good friend and ally Theresa Gooda, whose skills and wisdom are always so appreciated. She has launched a collection of poems recently, *Silence & Selvedge*, available at https://www.theresagooda.co.uk. I was thrilled when she asked me to illustrate the cover.

I am fortunate to have a brilliant team around me: our readers Catherine Lloyd, Alexandra Plowman and Karen Furse. They have been with me from the beginning of the Thrown Away Children series and I value their skills and insight so much. Jane Graham Maw is my very special agent who never fails me and offers constant sound advice. Thank you. Thank you also to my editor, Jo Sollis, (who is a kind editor and not at all scary) and to Claire Brown and the Mirror PR machine who help me bring my books to their wonderful audience.

Mostly I thank you, my readers, especially those I have regular conversations with. Fiona, you often make me laugh.

Thank you.

Help and Information

I am the founder of Spark Sisterhood. The traditional goodbye-and-good-luck approach for girls leaving care is outdated. It leaves girls vulnerable to cycles of struggle and adversity, incl. social exclusion, homelessness, unemployment, drug abuse and other challenges. We're here to change that narrative. With our employment pathways, mentoring program, community and online learning platform, we're reshaping post-care experiences for girls across the UK.

Website: https://www.sparksisterhood.org
Email: louise@louise-allen.com

My essential 'must haves' to support with foster care FosterWiki is designed to help empower Foster Carers with knowledge, through examples and experiences of other Foster Carers.

Website: https://fosterwiki.com/
Email: info@fosterwiki.com

COMING SOON
A BRAND NEW LOUISE ALLEN SERIES

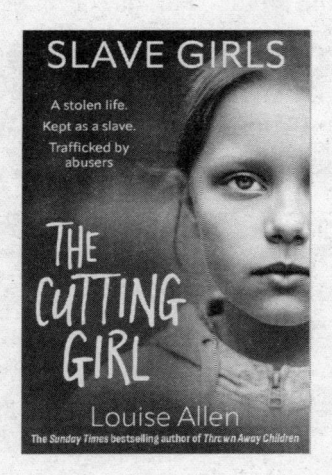

SLAVE GIRLS
Louise Allen
with Theresa McEvoy

Charlotte - The Cutting Girl - comes from a family of high achievers. Her father is a politician, and her mother is a senior medical officer.

When she moves from her prestigious boarding school she is groomed by a girl two years her senior, spiralling into a cycle of drugs, self-harm and sexual abuse.

When she goes missing, five other girls do, too. A nationwide media campaign sets out to track them down, but can Charlotte ever escape the gang behind the abduction and abuse?

I now foster with Fostering UK. A growing number of foster agencies are owned by private equity companies with the sole aim of making money. This has never been the intention of Fostering UK, and never will be.

  Website: https://fosteringuk.org.uk/
  Phone: 0333 044 8890

Finally, the National Union of Professional Foster Carers (NUPFC) provides valuable assistance and services to its members, including representation during the allegations process, representation during standard of care proceedings, as well as helping to find solutions to problems that may occur between you and your foster agency or local authority.

  Website: https://nupfc.com/
  Phone: 0800 915 1570
  Email: enquiries@nupfc.com